UPSURGE

Wreckage to Triumph, Rebuilding Your Personal and Business Life

Tab Pierce

UPSURGE Wreckage to Triumph, Rebuilding Your Personal and
Business Life

DEDICATION

There are many, many people to whom I am deeply grateful to for their assistance in writing this book. They have pushed me, bugged me and cajoled me to write. Thank you. To the many who were there to buoy me up, believe in me and support me through the years of hardship. Thank you. To my dear mother, who loved me unconditionally and passed away while I was writing, and who never saw this finished product. Thank you and I love you.

To a Father in Heaven who gave me life and a desire to achieve and excel. Any thanks I give to Him pale in comparison to what I owe. However, a heartfelt and humbled thank you.

To those that beat on me, pressured me and pushed me to pay debts, often in the most ruthless ways, I thank you. I thank you for taking me through the Refiner's Fire.

To my son Jackson for being there every step of the way as we bailed the company out together. Your belief and support is extremely humbling. I give you a very hardy and humbled thank you. To all my children, their spouses and my grandchildren, thank you for the support and giving me many days of smiles when I most needed them.

Last, and most important, is Catherine, my wife. She does not get enough credit for what she has been through, what she has supported me with and how much she took on and internalized as we worked through things together. She is the strongest person I know. Meek and humble, but an emotional powerhouse and with capabilities beyond anyone I know. You stayed with me, side by side. We are an eternal team. An eternal power couple. A dynamic duo. I look at you and my heart races, I look at you and see the same amazing girl I met 33 years ago. I see the one person that makes me feel like I won the lottery anew every single day. Thank you, and I love you.

CONTENTS

ACKNOWLEDGMENTS

Catherine Pierce helped me unceasingly during the writing of this book, always there and always willing to help.
John Avila who nagged and cajoled me regularly to finish and write
Gene Takashima for reading early chapters and providing me feedback

FOREWARD – MICHAEL BOSWORTH

Author of best-selling books, "Customer Centric Selling, Solution Selling and What Great Salespeople Do."

I first met Tab Pierce in 2015 when he and his sales team attended one of my Story Seekers® Workshops. Tab was an engaged leader and sales professional looking to find an edge for him and his team to use within their difficult selling market. Unbeknownst to Tab at the time, his company's issues had already started to set in before he attended the workshop. Over the following years, Tab has endeared himself to me and has become a true friend.

On occasion we met for lunch, and often spoke about his company's issues and how they have affected him on a personal level. We discussed at length his push to drive revenue, to increase sales, and his desire to use that to pay down his company debts. He was highly focused on raising sales acumen and subsequently improving revenue. Over that time, I saw his approach as a leader grow. I was privileged to watch him overcome his financial troubles and turn his company from a mess to success. I saw him harden in that leadership role, but more than anything I have seen him grow on a personal level.

During those lunches Tab would dig deep, asking me questions to further his knowledge about my Story Seeker Leadership and Customer Hero Selling and Marketing programs. Although a seasoned and experienced sales and business leader, Tab was curious and interested in the best practice ideas I have collected that could, and subsequently did, move his company forward. I'm confident it was that thirst for knowledge and his perseverance that led his company back from the brink.

Tab is a good storyteller. Tab tells his story well. From the discovery that his business had financial issues, all the way through to where it is today as a thriving business. However, it's that middle part where I believe you will gain the most significant insight. It's Tab's remorse, vulnerability, and doubt, all centered on his knowledge that the issues were his creation. It's Tab's willingness to be open about all the steps he took to leave that vulnerability behind and transition to a formidable and faithful person, who believed in his own ability to rebuild his business. Tab doesn't approach this as many do when they teach you how to be successful—from a point of strength. Instead, he allows you to see and feel that vulnerability and to take the journey of recovery with him.

I hope you enjoy his journey, that you learn, that you allow him to take you on the tour, and that you will be inspired by the hope, healing, and recovery throughout the pages.

Michael Bosworth

FOREWARD – WARREN SAMEK

Friend, Business Leader, Venture Capitalist

This is the story of an American Entrepreneur. This is Tab's story. And even though he made it through to the other side, he has decided to reach back and pull others through the fire by helping them make their own fire.

If you are an entrepreneur, business leader, or sales professional that's facing great adversity, then this book will offer you a safe harbor from the daily storm. You will find rest and mental restoration when you read **Upsurge,** for it will give you a shield and a sword, to hold the demons chasing you at bay. Demons disguised as creatures such as debt collectors, doubters, creditors, shame, sales quotas, customer rejection, governmental authorities, self-loathing, and a host of other animals gnawing at your mind all day and all night.

This book will also help you to understand the mother of all demons: self-doubt. Tab's **Upsurge** sheds light on understanding this demon, speaking her language and turning her into a useful guiding voice instead of the energy sapper she likes to be. When this book isn't acting as your sword and shield, it will be your friend, your umbrella, and your adult binky at night (or day).

I measure the value of my relationships in my life by what I can learn from them. Tab Pierce has taught me much over the years and continues to do so with this book. One of my favorite lessons from the book is the concept that "before you market yourself to others, you must market you to you." This concept is both rich and multi-layered, and crucial for success out in the real world. It's worth unpacking and Tab does a good job in breaking this concept down. People can sense your energy, your confidence, and whether you really believe in what you are communicating. We all have moments of self-doubt and having the mental model and tools to remind yourself of what makes you great is a healing and empowering capability that you must master.

Another idea in the book that resonates with me as both an entrepreneur and a veteran executive of the tech and finance industries is the simple concept of momentum. I won't offer a spoiler, but I will offer this phrase from the book that I think is just awesome: "Your momentum needs you". It certainly does, and it is a precious thing that we all have the capability to create. But the challenge is in sustaining your momentum and prioritizing your opportunities. Tab will show you how to build and sustain momentum through Opportunity Pipelines. The concepts are delivered in an easy-to-understand way, and in easy-to-digest bites of knowledge.

The concept of guarding your calendar is one of the most important skills (and attitudes) that this book illustrates effectively. Not being the master of your time is a common affliction in the age of always-on, always-connected devices and media. The idea of identifying the usual suspects which steal your time was also helpful to me as I read Upsurge. There are simple tools and powerful time management systems that can help you allocate your time, energy, and attention to what really matters. This one improvement alone can be life changing both personally and professionally. There is power in intelligent and intentional focus, and Tab offers some perspectives and recipes for allocating time and focusing your mind.

Undaunted. Many words can be used to describe Tab Pierce but the one that I like the most is **undaunted**. I've watched and heard many people tell Tab he couldn't do something or that a particular plan wouldn't work. I've always admired his response to these situations. You see, it's not that Tab does or doesn't believe them. I think many times he believes THEY believe what they're telling him. But Tab believes in himself, and he is reinforced and re-energized by his family and his faith. Additionally, Tab has a wonderful sense of adventure so if he did believe the people telling him he can't do something, well he's just going to try anyway to see what happens.

Science may have stolen many of our miracles but Tab likes to extract a self-made miracle—sometimes out of necessity, and sometimes just for fun. Tab writes with a voice of passion, pragmatism, and invigoration. He dispenses practical advice, often with humility and a sometimes painful vulnerability. His writing at times also has the tone of a war-weary victor who won the game playing it straight-up and honestly. The act of writing his story and putting himself "out there" struck me as a courageous effort to help comfort those that are going through inner turmoil, external tumult, and the same tribulations that Tab endured while building his business.

Tab has always tried to do "good" while doing "well", even when facing great struggles. Not only is this admirable, but it is essential for all of us to do to survive, thrive, and gain critical positive energy when it's needed most. Doing good with selfless acts, and having an attitude of selfless service in general, is invigorating and offers a special energy that can be harnessed to heal and endure and strive.

Tab never wanted to be glorified for being something that I find is precious and rare these days. Tab is a strong man of honor, of faith, and a great husband and father. This seems to be so hard to achieve in this day and age, and yet he downplays accolades regarding these admirable qualities. He values those qualities greatly but doesn't anchor his identity solely on his personal achievements and his strong character. He just figures maybe we should all be that way. Is he infallible? Are any of us? Read his book to find out a secret that I wished I had learned much earlier in life. His book is as much about having faith in yourself as it is about fighting fear. With Upsurge he gives you the ***"5 magic pills",*** a super supplement for your mental state and your mental strength. The chapter on "Thoughts" is fascinating and if you only have time to read one chapter this is the one you might pick.

I believe God puts people into other people's lives for a reason. When you read this book, you will bring Tab into your professional life...and you'll be glad you did.

Warren Samek

PRELUDE

What a ride the years leading up to this book have been. They were fraught and filled with fear, vulnerability and much fatigue. They were also filled with growth, determination, fortitude and discovery. In writing this sentence I'm filled with overwhelming gratitude for the experience, while at the same time deeply wishing I had never experienced it, and even more so wishing that I will never experience anything like it again. The years have left me stronger and more resilient than I ever knew was possible—in fact, I thought I was resilient until everything broke wide open. That's when the shallowness of my self-worth and value showed through, like car headlights coming right at me.

Then, bam! It all hit me.

In being open about all the business failures, struggles, doubts and fears, and equally open about my own self-worth and feelings of being a failure, fraud, vulnerable and polarizing fear I found an audience of quiet and relieved allies experiencing many of the things I had. They had just chosen to keep it to themselves out of shame. Shame was something I felt too, but it never kept me back from telling my story, even as I was living it. For that I am extremely grateful. Keeping all of this bottled up would mess with anyone's mental health and have them spiraling out of control.

It may seem like I am simply repeating myself when I talk about my professional and personal fears—but I have learned over time that I need to separate the two. I had to learn that my business was not me. I could feel a certain way about the business, and I could feel a certain way about myself, but they were two very different entities. Both needed healing and healing simultaneously. At times, the lines of which one I was healing and working on became blurred. Over time I learned to see the difference and being able to feel two different ways about the same thing. The business could be in pain and I was fine, or vice versa over the same thing. And that was okay.

That audience of people I found that was living through what I had lived through were relieved in knowing that they were not alone. And in sharing my story, in helping them and listening to them, I found my desire to help others at a level I was previously unaware of.

My hope is that this book can transcend business and help people in their personal lives too. If you are a homemaker but deeply troubled and in need of recovery, I hope you find an ally in these pages. If you are a successful CEO with a major company, but feel shallow and beaten and questioning, I hope through this you find recovery. If, like me, you are a small business owner who wakes up one day and realizes that you have royally screwed up and your entire value sinks to near nothing, I hope you find solace in these pages. Whatever your situation, no matter how alone you feel, I hope you can find something in this book that will help you. But most of all, I hope you find an ally.

When you are in the middle of the storm it's difficult to see the clear skies of the future. You spend all your time with your head down, literally and figuratively. When living a very difficult life it's hard to see any possibility of hope, and it seems like there are few options for an exit. In reality, the only thing keeping you back from creating possibilities and enjoying life in the middle of this storm is you. It's all you.

My assumption is that in reading this you have chosen one of two thoughts when I say it's all on you. The first is, "Yes, of course it's all on me." The second is, "No, you don't know what has gone on in my life, it is definitely not on me." Whichever you choose, you will still find the journey challenging. If you are already aware that you need to own your mistakes then you are part way there, but the journey to recovery and reinventing your life, career and business will be a great challenge. If you believe that it's definitely not on you or that there is plenty of blame to go around, then you will need to have an awakening to the fact that only you can take ownership over your own life. That's a hard pill for many to swallow. I hope you will keep reading, and realize like I did how empowering and liberating owning your mistakes is.

If you are picking this book up looking for immediate hope, salvation and recovery, that most likely won't happen. However, there are a few pills I can provide you quickly that will give you an enormous head start. If I had focused on these lessons earlier, then my business recovery might not have been any quicker but my personal recovery and how I viewed my business would have improved much faster.

Pill One

Gratitude has a way of leveling life out. It may not solve everything, but if you play the gratitude game long enough then you will find yourself unable to remain fraught with worry and fear. It is a battle though, one you must be willing to persevere through. Simply take the time to think of ten things you are grateful for. If you have a close friend or family member have them play with you. My wife and I would go back and forth stating something unique in an effort to build our gratitude muscle. At times the fear was so strong that we would need to break it down into sets of ten. What were we thankful for in our marriage? What were we thankful for in our businesses? What were we thankful for with our health? What were we thankful for with our spirituality? Gratitude will defeat fear if you are willing to focus on where you are truly thankful.

Pill Two

You have so much more power than you realize. You may think that since you are in such a low place, with no sense of self-worth that you have no power. Bu the truth is, when you hit rock bottom you have all the power. You have nothing to lose. As you read on and hear my story, you will learn that at one point my company owed money to 18 different people, businesses and government agencies. I felt beholden to nearly every one of them, and completely powerless. The truth was that I held the power, not them. If they wanted their money, they had to accept what I was able to do, and I decided what I was able to do. That power is within your reach. When you have little to lose, you have much to gain and the power to do that is within your grasp.

Pill Three

Your ability to change your outcome by changing your thoughts is an amazing practice. You can change your mood from second to second or minute to minute, without much thought. Imagine what you can do if you practice mindful thought? Realize that what you consciously tell yourself, the way you speak about situations, others, yourself and everything else matters. You need to guard your thoughts. Your conscious mind relays information that your subconscious mind uses to solve problems. It is estimated that 90% of your thinking time comes from your subconscious and only 10% is conscious. Your subconscious mind never shuts off. What you think matters, so change your thoughts from negative to positive now. You will learn that positive thought matters, but that alone will get you only so far. But for now, work on improving your thoughts.

Pill Four

Learn to meditate daily and as often as needed. Meditation comes in a lot of different forms, and you need to find what works and resonates for you. For me, I find that if I choose to meditate for 15 minutes the first 10 minutes is something like trying to get a toddler to lie down for a nap when they are not tired. I fight it, argue with myself, call it stupid and remind myself that I have real things that need to be addressed. This, however, is not one of them. It's that last five minutes that can make it all worthwhile. It's where I become centered and grounded. There are ways that I have grown with meditation and can center myself more quickly. Like everything, it's a muscle we develop and hone, and meditation can immediately impact you if you have the patience to preserve.

Pill Five

Thinking time, which is different than meditation, can help you create a foundation for making the right decisions. Often, we hurry to come up with a solution to a problem. You must learn that although others may see your need to respond quickly, you have the time to formulate good decisions. There are times that taking time to think allows all those random, fuzzy thoughts to align into something usable. Learning to make time for good thought can change your trajectory.

Final Thoughts

My hope for you as you read through this book is that you will find the ability to expedite your recovery quicker than I could. I hope that you will take what I've learned over these years and consolidate what you need to do, get to where you need to go and do it without the slow learning curve I experienced. However, should you need the time to do it as I did, know that there is great value in learning and working slowly and that you may find wisdom through this.

But mostly, I hope you see that you are not alone. That there are an army of individuals out there feeling vulnerable . That's my vision for the future; to create a community of people who go through this with others, graduate into superhuman recovery and growth, and then come back and help the next generation of people that stumbled and are trying to recover. They will be united in strength, beyond the recovery, and they will grow together.

I will always do my best to help you, the reader. As I write this, there are no issues with my being flooded with requests for my time, but ideally that will change! That means that this book, the content and what we want to build as a community has taken off. You can reach me at tab@tabpierce.com and I will do my best to help you to help yourself. But that's what this all comes down to—your ability to own your situation and to pull yourself out of it.

At the conclusion of each chapter I provide you with more pills that will allow you to consider ways you can take that information and impart it into your life. I hope you take the time to contemplate each and how they can be used to your benefit.

1 LOST AND FOUND

Written by Catherine Pierce

Tab asked me to write this chapter because he was mostly unaware of how much I held in to support him in what he was going through. My emotional support meant that I was left with little to no emotional support for myself. Tab wasn't being selfish; I was being strong for him. My hope is that I can provide some insight into how a significant other can support someone going through something like this.

Tab and I have been married for 33 years this year, and we've experienced a lot together. Most of the times have been great over the years, but the window between 2015 – 2019 was especially hard. Not only did we face financial strain but having to watch Tab go through everything he went through was crushing.

We made the choice early on that I would stay home and be there for the kids, and Tab would provide financially for our family. We did fine, and we were willing to forgo being a two-income family to ensure that I could be there for the kids. So, even though the trouble with Tab's business really "hit the fan" in 2016, there were warning signs before that.

See, Tab is a fun guy to be around. He is very quick-witted and has a way of putting people at ease from the very first moment they meet. He is very snarky. He has always been good at leaving the stress of work at the front door. He has made it a point to be present for me and the kids when he gets home. He has always been so self-confident. Not in a bad way—he's always been one to set goals and accomplish them. But in the couple of years before "everything hit the fan" his confidence started taking a gradual down-turn, and I noticed it long before he did. I am certain that his loss of confidence was the initial indication that the business was losing traction. The normally optimistic man that I loved, who usually made me laugh every day, began to be more stressed out.

That's what I noticed first. He was super stressed when he came home from work. He wasn't present anymore; he was impatient, and he would get easily irritated and stay that way for hours. It was completely unlike him; he hardly ever got mad about anything. The warning flags became clearer when we started missing paychecks. He would usually wait to say anything to me about us not getting paid on time until a few days before we would normally get the check. It was super stressful for me because at the time I was the one managing our family budget and honestly, I wasn't that great at it. We didn't have a lot of savings, which added more pressure. I remember getting frustrated that everyone in the company was getting paid, but we weren't. I told Tab, "If you know we aren't going to get paid on our normal paydays can you please tell me as soon as you know so I can be prepared?" He said that he would. I am sure each time that happened that he was hoping something would come in and he wouldn't have to give me bad news.

It couldn't have been easy to have those conversations about missing paychecks with me. Even though I tried to be strong and not worry about money in front of him, every once in a while, I would break down and tell him how hard it was to be so financially unstable. We didn't live extravagantly by any stretch. I just wanted to be able to pay our bills on time.

I vividly remember the day he came home after having the conversation with his accountant. He was a completely broken man. He wouldn't eat and hardly talked, which is rare for him. I had never seen him like this before, and I was worried sick about him. He would come home from work, sit in front of the T.V. and hardly say two words to me. He wasn't one to watch T.V., which gave me even more cause to worry. I had no idea what to do. I would ask him to talk to me, but at that point he couldn't.

What I didn't know was that all he could do was imagine the various different scenarios of how bad it could get. One night he told me that he thought he was going to go to jail. How would he be able to face our family? How would I provide for the family in his absence? I hadn't worked outside the home since 1989. I didn't have a college education to fall back on either. Later we learned that there was no possibility of him going to jail for this. It was just his anxiety running wild.

When he did finally open up and talk to me about how bad the situation was, I felt like I had been punched in the stomach. But I didn't let it show. I tried to reassure him that he wasn't going to end up in jail, and we would figure out a way to make everything work. I started driving for Uber. It was perfect for me, because I could be home when needed and work as many hours as I needed to. Driving in Seattle when I didn't know the city very well was awful. I am so grateful for navigation apps! Tab began to drive Uber during the weeknights and on the weekends. It sucked not having any time together, but we needed the money. He would put in long hours at work trying to figure things out and keep the business going. Then he would come home, grab something to eat, and turn around and drive Uber for five or six hours. He was exhausted and couldn't see the light at the end of the tunnel. Neither of us could.

It was like he was walking around with a storm cloud over his head, like on the anti-depressant commercials. I tried to remind him that he was more than his business, but he couldn't see that. He had tied all of his self-worth to his business's success. I tried to be strong for both of us. I encouraged him to tell me what was going on inside his head, hoping that would help, but it didn't.

When he met with the attorney who directed him on what to do to get things under control it helped some. But even as the months passed and he made progress with paying down the taxes and making arrangements with the hard money lender, his outlook really didn't change that much. It wasn't until 2019 that he started to gain his confidence back. He fought for it every step of the way. He spent countless hours working on his mindset, thoughts, and belief in himself.

Tab is different now. The process of working his business out of the terrible mess it was in has made him a stronger version of himself. He has an unwavering belief in himself that he can overcome anything. He has fought his way back from being lost to a new level of mental toughness, clarity and resilience that he has never had before. I am not the only one who recognizes it either; everyone can see it in the way he carries himself, his actions, and in the strength and encouragement he brings to others.

Situations like ours can easily drive two people apart, but it doesn't have to if you are willing to communicate clearly with each other. Even though you may be carrying the majority of the burden, be aware that your partner is also going through this with you and probably has no idea just how bad the situation is. Think about how hard and helpless they feel as they watch you experience everything you are going through, and not be able to do anything about it.

We had a great marriage before all of this happened, but it is even better now. Today we work together in our businesses and we are growing together. I could have pointed fingers at him, and I would have had every right to. But I decided to help him rebuild himself, and along the way I managed to strengthen myself as well.

2 TELL ME, WHAT IS IT WE DO?

This is a cautionary tale to be used in business and in life. My intent is to impress upon you that if an average, everyday knucklehead like me can get out of the trouble I got myself into, then you can do it too. There is hope. There is light. There is strength, and most importantly there is a level of growth you can gain by sticking with your problems and overcoming them. Let that last part sink in, because it is the weak that jump and bail, who look for the chance to exit and move on. In truth, that happened. I don't blame them; this was my mess and mine to clean up.

Here's the beautiful thing—it's only now that I have this peace of accomplishment, a sense that I can accomplish anything if I'm willing to focus and wait it out. That "it" could be anything. And as I type this, the overwhelming gratitude I have for the three years of hell covers me with warmth. Now, let me be clear about something. People who say if they had to do it again they would due to what they learned are totally full of crap. They're lying to you and to themselves. How do I know? Simple. I will do everything I can moving forward to never experience that again. Now I ask better questions of myself and listen closely to those that advise me so that I never have to go through this again.

In April 2016, my then Corporate Accountant, now Vice President of Operations, came to me with a question that led to the following conversation:

"Can you tell me what it is we do as a company?"

A little off put, my first thought was, "You should know the answer to that question." However, I went along with it and provided my response.

"We offer our clients a holistic security experience. We provide services that range from security testing their mobile and web applications to assisting them with governance, risk and compliance needs. Plus, we offer our platform to assist our clients with managing those needs on an ongoing basis."

Or at least my response was something like that, I used to have this really awesome canned delivery that sounded amazing to me.

His response startled me and started my exit from my state of denial. "Actually, that's not what we do at all. Eighty eight percent of our business comes from security testing services and staff augmentation. Only twelve percent comes from the majority of what you tell people. And that twelve percent is sinking this company."

My denial ran deep as I kept pushing on with what I felt was his misunderstanding of our overarching security posture. "It's not sinking our company, we're just not profitable with it yet."

"What you see as not profitable yet is actually a team that's draining resources we don't have, with no end in sight."

Fighting the good fight, I responded with, "That's not entirely true, if you look at what we have in the pipeline…"

He cut me off. "If we don't fix this now there won't be a pipeline. We have a real issue we need to address now. I need you to sit down, listen, and let me show you our financials."

Finally, Communication and Listening

Begrudgingly, I sat down and allowed him to plead his case, even as I was preparing to prove my own. As we moved forward through the discussion my mood changed from irritation at being told we were close to death to one where I had a repeating "Oh crap" moment followed by fits of despair. What he had been trying to relay to me for months was finally starting to sink in.

Yes, months. I had been oblivious to his every effort to impress upon me the dire reality of our position, and now it was all starting to sink in. Through months of him trying to relay and impress upon me our dire position and my being oblivious to his efforts it all started to sink in.

"Why hasn't this been brought to me earlier? Why didn't you tell me this early on when we could have stemmed the tide?"

It's so easy to view my plight and wonder how I could have been so stupid. Why didn't I see it coming? A friend and peer said to me later, "I couldn't believe you were so careless to allow that to happen." Then, it happened to me, but threefold.

Getting Real with Where We Were

I had finally accepted the reality of the company's debts. Talking about it now is easier because it's in the past, but it's still a level of vulnerability I have a hard time with. I do it because I believe it can help you. Seriously, it sounds cliché to say that, but I really hope my story helps you. That being said, these mistakes were mine, I made them, and I owned them.

These numbers aren't exact, but we owed roughly $750,000 to eighteen different government agencies, businesses and individuals. That was a colossal amount for a small company.

Things got much worse before they got better. It led to deep and heated discussions with one of my minority business partners. Accusations flew and fingers were pointed. It led to internal dissent and hostility that split our team, and that same owner forewent his ownership in lieu of departing with no legal recourse or obligation financially. It was ugly and painful.

This battle went on for months. When everything settled, we lost half of our leadership team. Along with myself, we reformed our leadership team into three of us, one being the other minority owner and the other my former corporate accountant and now new Director of Operations.

Closing the Doors or Fighting the Fight

While working through my management team challenges and mounting debt, the majority of advice I was getting was to close the doors, file personal bankruptcy and start again. Do something else, just not to waste my time trying to solve the current business troubles. That sounded great, just walk away. No harm. No foul. Except, it wasn't that easy.

Roughly, $250,000 of that debt was owed to the Internal Revenue Service. They would be as sympathetic as they needed to be. Which would have sounded something like, "Hey, we're sorry things didn't work out and you had to file bankruptcy. So, when do we get our money?" The IRS doesn't forgive your debt when you file bankruptcy. That chunk of change stays with you until you pay it back.

This was my dilemma, what was my best way of paying the IRS back? What was my largest and most painful challenge?

The answer to both questions was my company.

Gaining Insight and Strength

Today, people talk about how admirable it was that I stuck with it to pay back all that debt, how I rose to the challenge and overcame it. Some of the people that suggested I pack it in and move on told me they knew I could do it. That's total crap. They didn't know I could, but I did.

It sounds great; it sounds like I picked up the sword and fearlessly went to battle . But that's not the whole truth. I was scared and trapped. I plodded along each day, hardly able to get to the office and with no energy to drive home. The thought of going in the next day plagued me nightly; I didn't want to sleep because sleeping meant I had to wake up and go back to the office. Five o'clock on a Friday would roll around and I would feel this tremendous relief that I could rest. But that would only last until Saturday morning, when I knew Sunday would be there soon and then Monday. It was brutal for a very long time. Very few people saw how deep my fear ran or how much I felt like a fraud. I felt like Smokey Robinson's song, "Tears of a Clown." People saw the smile; they didn't see anything else.

We continued because we didn't have a choice—or at least, I didn't feel like I did. That's not the image of a warrior going to battle. I had the energy to show up, but not to lift the sword.

An interesting thing starts to happen to us in times of strife. Whether we realize it or not, we start to harden. We start to realize we have power that we haven't tapped, and it starts to come out of us, even as we are unaware. Each day I continued, and as hard as it was, I became that much closer to the sword carrying warrior others saw.

Discovery of a Mentor and Direction

During all of this, I attended a three-day conference with my Director of Operations. One of the speakers was Tim Grover, who I had discovered just months early but had become fascinated with. Tim's book *Relentless* had started to help me feel like I could be a warrior; that I could overcome many of these issues still facing me. Tim had given me hope. I had read and listened to his book several times by the time we attended the conference. Each word was as if he was speaking directly to me.

Tim asked for a one-hundred-dollar bill from the audience, which someone provided. He held it up, showed the eight thousand attendees and then put the money on the ground, stepped on it, crumpled it and did what he could to make that bill unsavory. He then picked up the mess and asked, "Anyone want this bill?" Eight thousand hands shot up. He then proceeded to ask us why? When we are treated like that bill by ourselves or by others, we devalue our worth. Aren't we more valuable than the bill? I did my best to keep it together, but that's what I was doing to myself, devaluing my worth due to the troubles I had created. I had allowed my company and the company's problems to define me as an individual.

As we sat over dinner at the airport my companion and I spoke about the conference. Much of the focus was around Tim's speech. My companion said, "You know if you could get over caring about how other people feel about you, stop judging yourself, and stop viewing what happened to the company as your identity, you would be unstoppable."

That was a turning point for me, both personally and professionally. It started to sink in, slowly at first as I processed how that would feel. I started to see what it would look like to be unstoppable. And over time, that vision moved from hope to belief.

On the flight home, I started to feel regenerated and capable. More importantly, I saw myself as believable. I was heading back home with my life healed and whole, ready to go.

Or so I thought.

Preparing for Battle

When we find the thing that heals us, we have such hope. We want to believe that the epiphany alone will bring us the salvation we desperately need. But life is more complicated than that—we don't simply learn our lesson and are suddenly complete. Instead, we are left to deal with the hurdles and obstacles that are in our way, and we must continue with that lesson for as long as it takes.

At this point, I was just under a year into salvaging my company, but it seemed much longer than that. What I didn't know was that I had a little over two more years of learning, experiences, growth and pain to endure.

The big difference now was that I had that discussion at the airport over dinner to replay in my head. It became my fuel. Each day I faced new and mounting challenges, and some days I reverted to my old ways of believing I was my company and I was my mistakes. But I became better at changing my thoughts and started to believe I could be unstoppable.

Pills

1. Who can you communicate clearly with about your current position and needs? Who is it you need to have these conversations with?
2. How can you prepare yourself to listen better so you can maximize your personal and organizational needs?
3. Take time to evaluate where you are. If in business, what happens if you close the business or decide to keep it open? Weigh the pros and cons of both. The same would be true if you are looking at a career change or significant personal matter.
4. Who do you have to mentor you? If you don't have one, who can you find that can guide you through this process?
5. Regardless of your decision on what to do you will need to prepare for battle. What can you do to prepare yourself for what comes next?

3 THE ROAD TO DEBT REPAYMENT STARTS WITH GOOD INTENTIONS

It's hard to put into words just how demoralizing and devastating that year was, or how difficult the next two years digging the company out of the hole I had created would be. At times fear gripped me, and I was constantly exhausted. We were one deal going south away from going under. Looking back, I wonder how close we really were. It still seems like we were always right there, on the edge.

There's one question I keep coming back to: was saving the business just luck, or were we actually good at it?

We had been hemorrhaging money and we were doing our best to make small payments on our debts where we could. Choosing to pay down friends and smaller debts first. Someone with more experience might think we made the wrong move, and maybe we did. But living through it, moment by moment, we made the decisions that felt right at the time. I forewent salary as much as possible and funneled those funds into paying down the debt. By this time, we had already used our funds in the previous year for various things from lowering debt to paying salaries. I was personally tapped out, financially and emotionally.

I sat down with my wife to discuss how we were going to bridge our own personal financial gap. Out of all the options—which included her getting a full-time job and me taking another job —we settled on us both driving for Uber. I had heard a lot of things from drivers about the pay, etc., but it helped us during that time and I'm extremely grateful for it.

While all of this was going on, my wife was the full-time caregiver to my mother. She would spend the day with my mother and drive at night. I would stay with my mom while my wife was out driving, then when she would get back, I would head out driving. Between running a business with no pay, two people driving Uber and both of us caring for my mother, stress and exhaustion ran high.

As much help as Uber turned out to be in bridging our financial needs, it caused me to further doubt myself. Afterall, I was the CEO who had built this company, grown it through two acquisitions of other small companies and had brokered major deals to provide our services to Fortune 500 companies. Now I was driving people around in my car making pennies on the dollar. Often when talking with a passenger conversation would turn to what else I did for work. As you can imagine, when they found out I was the CEO of a company they always had questions, which only reopened the wounds.

Defining Our Debt Repayment Direction

We had to determine which debts we would pay straight away and which we would sit on. No one was getting their money fast enough. The more we dove into revenue generated versus debt to be paid out, along with funds needed to sustain business, the more we realized the mounting issue we had before us. How do we determine who to pay and who had to wait? How could we forecast funds throughout the process? Should we take an aggressive approach to paying people off based on a belief we could increase revenue?

Here's the thing—when you are in trouble like this and you have people hounding you for money, it's easy to shrink and hide. One way to do that is to over promise and under deliver. It's not as if you set out to be deceitful; you just want to ease your pain and lower the blow that's being inflicted upon you by people.

Don't.

You must be realistic, and you need to be honest with all your creditors about your current situation.

There's a logical way to go about paying off large sums of debt—the trouble lies in the emotional side of things. If all creditors were created equal, paying down debt would be easy. They're not. Amongst the eighteen creditors we had government agencies, a hard money lender, vendors, attorneys, reimbursements to employees, contractors, friends and others. Some had steep interest rates and penalties, some were adept at threats and pressure, others were friends just trying to help friends out and there were a few that were like leeches that I just wanted to be done with. That mix made the decision to pay down the debt an emotional one, and not just based on logic. It is extremely painful when you speak to someone and say they're not going to get their money as planned.

The Emotional Side of Debt Repayment

The Pareto principle, or the 80/20 rule, is the rule of the vital few. In sales, it means that 80% of your revenue comes from the top 20% of your clients. It could also mean that 80% of your problems come from 20% of your clients. For us and our debts, it meant that 80% of our most painful and aggressive pushback and threats were coming from three or four creditors. That's not to say pushback didn't come from the others, but those few were much harder to handle.

Looking back, I'm glad we handled the debt the way we did. We covered those closest to us first; our friends and the contractors that were impacted. From there we became much more logical about how and who we paid. In my mind I created a line of people, 18-people deep that went around the block. Some, I could see their faces because I knew them personally, while others were just fuzzy figures. Of course, there was restlessness and impatience; everyone had to wait. Even our friends waited as no one was getting their money as originally planned. That's the way it worked out. It's not a point in my history that I look back on in satisfaction, though I am still glad we paid people back instead of filing bankruptcy.

Friends who expected payment in full on a certain date had to accept weekly payments over an extended period. Reimbursements were delayed. Contractors had to wait. Their patience often ran thin— sometimes, extremely thin. Remember, these are the people that liked us, or at least, had liked us at one point. We're not talking about businesses or government agencies at this point. Tempers were often frayed, and complaints or threats were made. At times I would have to tell someone that if they pushed too hard, no one was getting their money back. I'd tell them to get back in line and wait. Well, except the IRS. I used the threat of bankruptcy as often as needed. It was one of the few leverage points we had at that point, and though I wasn't willing to go through with it I okay with using it to keep people at bay.

Each step of the process was personally difficult for my wife and me. Having to tell friends who trusted us that we couldn't meet the original agreement and they had to agree to something else in order to get anything back was hard. What kind of person was I that would put my friend's money in jeopardy? More importantly, what kind of friendships did I foster?

Embarking on the Process of Paying Down Our Debt

Here's a tip: when you set out to take a conservative and realistic approach, assume it'll take you three times as long.

We developed a plan to repay people and set out to perform

according to the outlined plan. Some received an outline of when they would receive payments, while we simply asked others for patience with the promise to repay them at some point. The latter, for the most part, wasn't received well. There were some that understood, and although they didn't like it, lived with it. The former, mostly friends, employee reimbursements and contractors were given a plan of repayment. We started with employees, contractors and then friends.

For the most part reimbursements went quickly, as did contractors. Most were smaller amounts, where we were able to see a clear ninety-day path to payment. Friends were more difficult. We had set out to pay them on a weekly basis once we were able to get past the others. This, however, wasn't a small amount and payments were missed as our conservative plan turned out to be not conservative enough.

Underlying all of this was a great deal of turmoil. It was a tornado of creditors calling to collect, internal leadership battles, legal issues around one owner leaving, dealing with the IRS, communicating with a hard money lender, and managing my personal finances and relationships. When I said Friday night was my weekend, that wasn't an exaggeration. It was the sole moment of the week that I felt peace and calm before the worry set in again.

The IRS and The Hard Money Lender

While we were dealing with the smaller, but more personal debts, we also had to manage repaying back taxes to the IRS and our decision to stop all payments to the hard money lender. Both were highly stressful.

Dealing with a hard money lender will never, ever, be a part of any business I'm involved with again. Even if you have the money coming in regularly, it's painful. The interest rate is high, and often the repayments are daily. At best, the relief only lasts a few days until that daily tick starts to happen from your checking account. It's a bad solution, regardless of the need. Can't pay employees? Figure it out, don't take out a hard money loan. That's based on when we were complying with the daily payments, which is nothing compared to how bad it got. But it's important to remember that I created that mess—not the money lender. I had to own that mistake, and so do you. It's important for you to own the mistakes you make, there's no better way to solve your problems and to grow as a leader than owning the bad along with the good.

It became clear that we couldn't make the daily payments to the hard money lender, pay back the IRS and meet all our other obligations. At the advice of our attorney we stopped all daily payments to the hard money lender. But a few days later they started again, just at a different amount. There was a loophole we didn't know about—they already had our permission to debit the account, and our block was only on that specific amount. So, we had to contact the bank and set a range from one cent to well over five figures in order to truly stop all future payments.

And then it started, the phone calls, the emails and the text messages. That's when it got rough. However, we had made the decision that we were going to wait them out regardless of the pressure until the IRS was paid off—which could have been years.

Letting them know of our plans to pay after our obligations to the IRS were fulfilled did no good in stemming the tide of threats. While there are certain laws that prevent moneylenders from taking action, they made sure to make as many veiled threats as they could. They often used other companies to reach out to us and make threats on their behalf. They went right up to the line of what was considered acceptable and legal, and I'm sure we could have argued that they crossed that line. The stress, worry and fear ran deep for a very long time. They were relentless for six months and then they were gone. They just stopped contacting us. The emails stopped. The letters stopped. The calls stopped. It all just stopped.

But not forever.

Learning to Love The IRS, If That's a Thing

With the IRS we had heard these stories about how ruthless they could be. We heard this from others with experience and we heard this from our attorney. The message was, don't take the IRS lightly. So, we didn't.

We went through meeting after meeting with our attorney. We provided countless documents that covered our financials and the legal structure of the business. They asked for documents that made no sense to me, but we provided them anyway. This went on for six to eight months, and the stress and worry mounted. Our attorney negotiated a repayment plan of $17,000 a month. My own internal accountant, the one I mentioned earlier, thought that amount was too steep and that there was no way we could make it and keep up with everything else. We were finally at the point where we were waiting to hear whether the IRS would accept our offer when word came to us that our attorney had been killed in a bicycle accident. What would that mean to our agreement? Where did we stand with the IRS? Do we start over with a new attorney? For a few days we just waited and wondered and pondered our course of action. Then our IRS revenue office called me. Up to that point I hadn't spoken with him directly, only with our attorney present.

"Hi, Mr. Pierce? This is Mr. Stewart your revenue officer with the IRS. Can we speak for a few minutes?"

"Uh, yes that's fine." At this point I was extremely nervous, but what could I say?

"I'm sure you've heard of the passing of your attorney?"

"Yes, very tragic. He was a good man and I had grown to like him immensely."

"We were all shocked to hear of his passing, many of us have worked with him for years. Have you engaged a new attorney?"

"Not yet, should we? It's something we've been discussing, but this is all so sudden and new."

"That's fully within your right. However, we have a window of opportunity to work directly before you engage another attorney. We're up to the goal line, I'm wondering if we can come to an agreement and punch this through?"

"Perhaps; it depends on what you are offering." For some reason I felt like I could bluff. That I could negotiate. I had no idea what was going on, I felt extremely vulnerable but felt the need to play it cool.

"Mr. Pierce, we have been negotiating your monthly repayment plan and frankly the numbers don't work for me." Here it goes, I knew as soon as I heard who it was, he was going to stick it to me.

"I don't see how $17,000 a month can work. Looking at your financials I believe you will default at that amount. I want to offer you a repayment much lower. Do you think you could do $10,000 a month?"

I wanted to ask if I was being trolled. Seriously, the IRS was offering a lower amount than what my attorney was asking for? That the negotiating back and forth between the two of them may have been the revenue officer asking for less and the attorney asking for more? To this day I can't get my head around that one.

"Well, I'm not sure what to say but yes! And that I am shocked that you would do that."

"Mr. Pierce, it does you nor the IRS any good if you default on payments. Speaking of defaulting, you can miss a few payments before we consider you in default."

"Well, what happens if we do default?" I felt my fortunes growing, why not ask questions to see how far I could push things if needed?

"We strongly suggest that doesn't happen, but if it does, we want you to keep making payments until we revisit it. That way it's easier for us to come back and create a new plan that meets your needs. At that time, we may revisit to an even lower amount."

"Well, we don't want to go down that road, but all information is good to know should the inevitable happen."

"Mr. Pierce, do we have an agreement? Can we move forward?

"Yes. Absolutely. And thank you!"

I hung up the phone, called my internal accountant and relayed the story. We both, in shock, felt we had finally gotten a break and some breathing room, and from the IRS at that. We had never seen them as an ally or willing to help us. They were evil and out to get us—but nothing could have been further from the truth.

Truthfully, they were amazing to work with. They deserve credit for helping small businesses get through hard times while recovering the funds that belong to the people. Over the years we had a few hurdles to cross with them, but each time they came into our office and assured us that we would make it through together if we were able to continue progressing. They acted more as a partner than they did as an enemy.

The takeaway for you is that should you find yourself behind on taxes to the IRS, you must communicate with them. Don't hide, but work with them. We would have saved time and money had we worked directly with them instead of through an attorney. Of course, your experience may be different—I'm not here to dole out legal advice! Just make sure that everyone is on the same page.

Dealing with The Hard Money Lender

After roughly eighteen months things were beginning to look up, and we were feeling comfortable that we were going to come out of this without much further difficulty. But the lack of communication from the hard money lender lulled us into a false sense of security. You should never tell yourself that just because someone has fallen quiet, they've gone away—especially if you owe them money. They showed up in our email, voicemail and text with a vengeance.

What they'd done previously was nothing compared to now. Not only were the email and letter threats stronger they started coming in all capitalized letters. It's a crazy tactic to talk to someone sternly, threatening and using upper case letters. Emotionally, it felt like a heightened attack.

There was new dimension to the threats: the fear they would show up at our offices. On two occasions they sent certified letters stating that they would be at our office with the local police department to seize our assets and arrest me for failure to pay the debt. I sent everyone home and waited, but they never showed. Not only did they send letters to the office, but also to my home address. They called my wife, my daughter, and my 87-year-old mother. Every day was spent in fear, and I eyed everyone that loitered outside with suspicion. It was relentless.

All the stress, worry and fear started up again. The only thing we could do at the time was to tell them we still weren't ready to deal with them. We needed them to wait eight more months before we could pay them. We had to stay with our original course of action, we could not deviate. After weeks of hard-core pressure, the communication stopped again. What was the deal with these guys?

I remember the day, I was taking a break and attending a day game at the Seattle Mariners. When I was checking my email in the middle of the game, I received a message from the hard money lender. "MR. PIERCE, YOUR EIGHT MONTHS ARE UP, PER YOUR

PREVIOUS EMAIL YOU SHOULD HAVE USED THAT TIME
TO PREPARE TO REPAY YOUR LOAN OBLIGATION.
SHOULD YOU DEFAULT AT THIS TIME WE WILL TAKE
LEGAL ACTION. THIS IS YOUR FINAL NOTICE. WE WILL
NOT NEGOTIATE FURTHER DELAYS. I AWAIT YOUR
IMMEDIATE RESPONSE. AGAIN, YOUR RESPONSE
CANNOT BE A DELAY, IT NEEDS TO BE YOUR PLAN TO
REPAY IN FULL."

My heart skipped a beat, and I passed the message on to my
accountant. We both knew it was time to pay up. We spent the next
few weeks formulating different plans to try and repay them without
putting us under too much strain. Unfortunately, no easy option was
available.

Finally, we settled on the least painful, but still very difficult,
agreement. We laid out an eight-month repayment plan that at times
felt like running a cheese grater over your head repeatedly. Those
eight months pushed us financially, strained the company growth,
and created a myriad of challenges. Week after week we struggled to
have the money for them. It felt like if we missed a payment, they
would show up to break our kneecaps.

The last month was brutal and we were almost tapped out, but we
were down to less than $20,000 owing—so long as we made the final
payments. If we missed a single payment, we would owe them six
times as much. For weeks we battled them, worked with them,
challenged and begged as we struggled to finally pay off the debt.

Finally, on July 18th, 2019 we made our last payment. We were debt
free at last.

Moving into the World of Sustainability and Beyond

Years of dealing with debt, saddled by fear, doubt, anxiety and
constant worry were gone. Just like that. It was an oddly surreal

feeling, a combination of disbelief and peace. We had done it. We had overcome what many people said we couldn't.

There are many things I've learned as we've come out of this debt, and many more I'll continue to relay in the coming pages of this book, but the first is that you have much more power than you realize. As painful as it may be, you can do what you must to achieve what you need. This is something I grew into overtime, and you will too.

There are three basic levels of business, which are true in life as well. We're either in survival, sustain or thrive mode. We can spend a lot of time in either survival or thrive mode, but we never stay long in the sustain mode; maintaining that level of equilibrium is just too hard. The difficulty comes when you leave either mode and move into sustain. Sustain is dangerous. Sustain feels a lot like the other modes. Sustain is trouble. At this point in time we were transitioning from sustain to thrive, but we had spent so long in survival mode that many of our actions were still set to ensuring survival. And without shifting to thriving, we ran the danger of falling back into survival mode.

Pills

1. If you have debt that's weighing on you, take time to outline where the money is owed and who gets paid back in what order. If possible, have someone in your business or personal life assist you.
2. From there, make a conservative plan that you can meet. At some point, you will need to relay that plan to creditors, but you will need to determine the timing of that for yourself.
3. Embrace the process and realize that you hold the power. While creditors want their money, you have your plan. Your action here is to keep the end in sight.

4. Identify the few people that can be there for emotional support, but do so realistically. You don't need a cheerleader; you need a coach.

4 CLARITY AND DIRECTION

My world was defined by fear and stress from long before my troubles began until long after they had subsided. However, I shouldn't have let it control me so. It's important that you learn quickly and early to control and change your thoughts and mood. Shifting your intentions towards abundance over scarcity is difficult, but essential. You must act on this daily—and not worry if you slip up and fall backwards. It happens, but the more we remove scarcity from our lives the greater we will prosper.

Choosing Fear or Faith

Fear and faith are both destinations, and in every area of our life we subconsciously make the choice to follow one or the other. We make these choices multiple times a day without even realizing it. For our subconscious to make faith the de facto choice, our conscious needs to actively feed thoughts of faith to our minds, and subsequently our subconscious mind. It takes a lifetime to become fearful, but it doesn't have to take the same to become faithful and live abundantly. It will take effort, energy, practice and patience. We will need to be persistent and pull ourselves back when we start to drift back to fear. This needs to be a conscious effort.

Many things would distract me, derailing my efforts and thoughts. Something would come up that needed to be addressed—often multiple times a day, week or month. They could be fleeting, or they could take a while to resolve. They often would be lumped together in my mind, becoming a tangled knot of problems. This would sit and fester until I convinced myself I was facing impending doom.

Sitting back one day, I thought: "I'm tired of always worrying. I don't have to do this. I'm making a choice to give my energy and time to this." I was giving my problems an extreme level of attention when no attention was needed. I focused on the wrong thing, bogging down and stalling growth. I was choosing scarcity over abundance.

We can choose what impacts us, and where we focus our energy and efforts. So, are you going to live faithful or fearful?

Bit Actors, Supporting Actors and You

As I sat there, I thought about the people and situations in front of me. At the same time, I scrolled through my contact list and landed on my contact at the hard money lender. I'd set it to be all in uppercase, because that was how his emails came—it amused me to see his name yelling at me when he called, but it caused me extreme anxiety. And then he was gone, disappeared when the loan was paid.

It hit me—that guy was a bit actor. He wasn't important in my life. Although he was in it for at least a year, I was giving him starring role status in my life when I didn't need to.

Think of your life as a documentary. You are the main actor; the star performer. You are what matters. You are the person who will always be there, which means you need to treat the star with the respect they deserve. Supporting actors are important too: these include your spouse or significant other, children, parents, family and lifelong and important friends. They are the people that enrich your life. Bit actors are people who show up for a day, week or a month and deserve none of our real attention; just a token amount of energy to manage them properly and respectfully. That's it, nothing more. I'm sure that if you tried, you couldn't remember all the people that had passed through your life. If you won't remember them in six months, why give them any more attention than you need to today?

To provide more clarity, I recorded these thoughts on bit actors on my smartphone so I wouldn't forget. As I dictated thoughts to word, I had mentioned three of the bit actors that were causing me discomfort. As I write this two of the three are gone, no longer even a bit actor! The bit actors in my life were just nuisances that, had I not changed my way of thinking, I would have given them more attention than they deserved. These bit actors are like a revolving door—one goes out, and another one comes in. To add even more insight, I write this sentence months later as I do a personal proof and edit before sending off for professional and final review. As I consider these particular bit actors, I have no idea who they were. I remember writing this, however I can't remember the situation. Even more fuel for our consideration on where bit actors should reside in our lives!

How Should we Handle Bit Actors?

We handle them by giving them only the energy that they need in order to reach the desired outcome. That's it. We don't become emotionally attached; we just do what needs doing. By choosing to live in faith, we assume the outcome will be good. By doing this, we're more likely to see things clearly and drive them to a quicker, more desirable outcome. So, when a bit actor comes into your life, just think; "They will be gone in a week. I'll give them the thought and attention they need, but they're not getting any more and they are not driving me to a fearful reaction."

Pills

1. Are you choosing fear or faith? Consider the thoughts that lead up to your decision. What thoughts and actions can you take to live in faith?
2. Who are the bit actors in your life? Can you list them and identify them?
3. With that list, can you determine how you will handle each bit actor?

5 GUIDING YOUR THOUGHTS FOR IDEAL RESULTS

Before we begin, let me preface this chapter by saying that I found this chapter particularly difficult to edit. I even considered completely redrafting it. It was the very first chapter I wrote, and I did so at a deeply emotional time. But ultimately, I decided to keep it as it is. Changing it would be a disservice to you, the reader, so that you can fully appreciate how vulnerable I truly was.

For many years I've been intrigued by how hard it is to control my own thoughts. They can take on lives of their own—for some people, to the point of fantasy. You may be thinking of people that fit that description right now. You know the kind; they are completely out of touch.

Guess what? This includes you.

Just hear me out and let me paint you a picture, one of me just a year ago. I read this now and can't help but think I was being melodramatic; I was in a very bad place emotionally and it was leaking into my thoughts in a big way. At one point my wife spent a week sitting in the same room with me and I was so preoccupied with my thoughts that I hardly said a word to her. Literally, sitting in my chair, so deep inside myself that I lost touch with what was going on around me. My thoughts were deep, dark and ugly. I wasn't suicidal, but I was more than willing to take my ticket and sit there and wait until my number was called and be done with life.

But then, for whatever reason, I had a good day. Maybe it was a good hour, I can't remember. During that time, I penned this simple note to myself in an attempt to rescue me.

This is For You, My Oft Wayfaring Friend.

I would like to visit you more often; I would like to remind you of who you really are. So, I wrote this letter. When you let me out, you let me feel the joy and happiness there is in life. When I'm allowed to enjoy time with good friends and family. When I'm permitted to love myself, to love Catherine, love my children, grandchild and mother. I have so much I would like to offer to you, I would like you to read this letter when you feel blue as a reminder to allow me to take part in your life. Do you remember when we were happy together? When we thought positively about us, our present and our future? Do you remember hope? Do you remember love? Do you remember peace and joy? I would like to help you find those again, and I would like it very much if you would allow me back into your life and we could work together to be all the things we knew we could. I still know what we can be, however I don't want to go anywhere without you. You are me and I am you, and we need each other.

So, here are a few things to remember.

1. *Love yourself because you are great, you are amazing, and you have unlimited possibilities*
2. *Your wife loves you and admires you, she can be an amazing resource*
3. *Your children love and admire you and can also be an amazing resource*
4. *You have great friends to support you, lean on them so they can lean on you*
5. *Life is beautiful, right here, right now.*
6. *Smile. Be happy. Have joy. Seek peace.*

7. *Remember what you have learned, push forward and seek the happiness you deserve*

8. *Focus on the positive, eliminate the negative and don't mess with Mr. in-between*

9. *It's OK not to be perfect and it's OK when people say hard things about you, but remember that you are much, much more than the few might see. You are greatness.*

10. *Mostly though remember that you can accomplish all things through Jesus Christ, Your Heavenly Father and the Holy Spirit.*

I want you to see what I see; I want you to feel the joy and peace I have. I'm desperate, I'll admit, because without you there is no me. That scares me. I, you and we need you to rise above the ashes and realize your amazing gifts and possibilities.

With love and devotion,

Happy Tab

A year later, there is one change Happy Tab would like to make to that last paragraph. I'm Tab, not Happy Tab. I don't need or want that other part in my life. Yes, good for me to remember so I can keep my joy and focus clear, but my thoughts are positive, and we kicked that oft wayfaring guy to the curb.

I also learned a valuable lesson along the way: I'm not my business. Business could be great, or it might be horrible, but that doesn't mean I'm either of those things. I needed to fix both my business and me, but they are two different things.

After I wrote this letter things continued to decline in a few key areas of my life, but my thoughts shifted positively, and this shifted a move towards improving. The stories we tell ourselves lead us in a direction, so make sure the direction they lead you in is in your best interests.

A Case for Realistic Thoughts

A word or two of caution: positive thoughts left unchecked can be dangerous. We're not talking about countering positive with negative, but with realistic thoughts instead. Each thought leads to an action, and if left unchecked and unbalanced may lead you into an action that's not favorable.

When my company experienced troubles and we determined a course of action we should have asked a few more questions of ourselves. Perhaps we could have asked, "If we do this, what could go wrong?" Maybe we could have asked, "If we don't do this what are the potential outcomes, and would those be worse than taking this action?" I believe with more realistic and well thought out discussions we would have made different decisions, ones that wouldn't have cost us a substantial amount of money and lost time. True, it would have been more difficult for us in the short run. We would have had an extremely painful and difficult six to twelve months. But instead we had a very painful and expensive three years.

Asking realistic questions and having clear thoughts that are void of emotions can help you make better decisions. If the action you are taking is important enough, consider having a committee help you formulate your ideas. Search out people with experience, those who can mentor you through the process of making the best decisions with your information. However, the ultimate decision must reside with one person, and most likely that person is you.

Being positive does not mean you charge ahead without checking yourself. You can positively say no. Again, no thought should go unchecked.

The Funny Thing with Thoughts

While having a discussion with a close friend about an event that happened years ago, we both vividly remembered details completely differently. Both of us were incredulous and found it hard to believe the other felt so strongly about something that was obviously wrong. We had to bring in others to help us remember what had happened. Who ended up being right? Both of us—but if you are a half glass empty kind of person, we were both wrong. We had entire locations wrong, people wrong and outcomes wrong. It was crazy that our perceptions of reality were off by the degree they were.

But not you, right? Ever know exactly where your car was left, only to find it not where you remember? How about finding out you like a food that for years you thought you hated? The thoughts we tell ourselves and our subsequent belief system can lead us in a direction, as if they were the Puppeteer and we're the puppet. It's maddening—or so the Puppeteer would want me to believe.

The other day, while watching a baseball game, a commercial for migraine medication came on and exclaimed that 8 out 9 sufferers of migraines noticed significant improvement. As I glanced to the small print at the bottom of the screen something caught my eye. I had to rewind it to make sure I saw it correctly. There it was in ultra-small print: 6 out 7 tested with the placebo noticed significant improvements too. Really? Those two outcomes are pretty much identical. One is 88.8% and the other 85.7%. If this was politics, we'd call that within the margin of error. What does that tell us? Our thoughts are real.

I can hear the critics now, "But Tab I really am in pain and by you saying it's in the thoughts of 6 out of 7 people you diminish my real illness." However, is that you talking or the Puppeteer? Illness is just an example. It could be us as parents, children, employees or about our weight, hair, wrinkles or any host of items.

This concept will either irritate you or fill you with visions of possibilities. That's a decision between you and the Puppeteer. Napoleon Hill said it best: "Whatever the mind can conceive and believe, the mind can achieve." There is a key word in that phrase, and that's achieve. We'll get into that more in-depth, but for now let's remember that to achieve means to carry something through. It means you've done something. This seems obvious, right?

We are bombarded with messages of positive thoughts being sent out to the universe with the result being that something shows up for us. I'm here to call crap. It's crap that all we need to do is think it. It's crap that positive vibes make it happen. It's crap that things just materialize. It's like ordering a pizza and thinking it into your mouth.

Thoughts, however, are where it starts. Glorious thoughts. Horrible thoughts. Apathetic thoughts. It all starts with our thoughts. Usually, the thoughts occur without us even thinking about it. Did you catch that? Without us thinking about it! The subconscious mind is so amazing that it provides the thoughts for you without effort on your part. How sweet is that? Maybe not. If your subconscious tells you that life sucks, it will lead you to a sucky life. Which of course sucks. You can teach your subconscious to tell you that life is amazing, which will lead you to an amazing life. Which of course is amazing!

Hard Times and Harder Thoughts

To be clear for a minute, there are times when very heavy and very hard things come our way; things that can make even the most positive of individual's knees buckle. Death, disease, betrayal and so on can cause us heartache and despair. That is the truth, cold hard truth. Even in those times the Puppeteer comes out to direct us. It's just natural.

But it's how we let it direct us in times of trouble that can define us. Lou Gehrig, in his heart wrenching speech to the New York Yankee fans on July 4, 1939, said: "Fans, for the past two weeks you have been reading about a bad break I got. Yet today I consider myself the luckiest man on the face of the earth." In his darkest days suffering from ALS his thoughts were directed to his fortunes, not his misfortunes. Our thoughts can and do direct us in the direction we desire.

Gehrig desired to be happy, he desired to leave a legacy. That legacy led many to see Lou Gehrig as the positive side to an ugly and debilitating disease.

When we have days that include flat tires, irritated spouses and angry bosses, our thoughts may lead us directly to, "What's next, what else will go wrong?" That thought will find a way to manifest itself into the next in a long line of suck. You thought it, you delivered it. Sucks, but what can you do, right?

You can take control of your thoughts. You can direct them. You can lead the charge to a positive outcome in the day, and ultimately, in your life.

Each day you are faced with moments that can either cause you irritation or happiness. The other day I pulled up to two lanes merging to one, everyone in the right lane knows it ends (or so I assume). My first thought was to accelerate and squeeze those bastards out! Alternatively, and what I chose to do, was to let them go first. Each irritant, each moment of happiness, you bank and withdraw at the end of the day. In a bad or good mood at the end of the day? Chances are it's based on a series of small decisions and actions taken throughout the day. Choose wisely.

Reaching a Positive State

Let's take a look at how we can reach that positive Zen of thought.

First, you need to come clean with yourself and admit you need to guide that Puppeteer instead of it guiding you. You will need to admit that in one way or another, more often than not, your thoughts are not aligned with your desires. Thoughts are and can be trained. They are either trained by you, managed by you or by the Puppeteer. That's your choice.

This is the point where I hear that people can't control what happens, they just do things or other's actions cause them to react a certain way. That's crap, and you should be happy it's crap. Excuses provide you with a way to opt out of life and allow you and your thoughts to run amok with whatever whim the day or moment may bring. It creates the suck you don't want, the suck you get and the suck you subconsciously gravitate toward. I know you don't want to suck. Consciously, you are correct. But subconsciously, you are embracing the suck. I'd love to say I never embrace the suck, but that's not true. Our life is full of moments and it's unrealistic to expect perfection. With all the thoughts and actions we generate in a day, we're occasionally going to suck. However, our goal should be to become unsuckable.

Thoughts are like muscles. If we use them right, we get stronger, we don't we turn to flab.

Secondly you need to have a desire to control and manage your thoughts. Some are going to be difficult, and others easier. The next time your teenage daughter yells at you you'll have an opportunity to yell back as usual, or stop, hear what she says and control the next words that come out of your mouth. That takes discipline, humility and patience and a willingness to become greater for both you and your daughter. Getting mad is easy, giving in and giving thought is hard. The great part is you have the choice. You can be in control.

Thirdly, there needs to be a plan. We all have triggers, things that set us off. If we plan to know what and when those things occur, we will be armed with an awareness in the midst of a trigger event. Planning requires regular and repetitive reviews of what events lay before us and a vision of how we want those events to play out. Reviewing events before we start the day and reassessing as difficult situations present themselves will help drive you in a positive direction. A long view vision of what you want to accomplish provides you with the clarity needed to reach those goals.

However, this isn't a light switch; it's more of a hand cranked water pump that constantly needs to be worked if you want the desired results. You pump, pump, pump and then water finally comes out after your arm is tired. Then, the next day you must start the pumping all over again. And so, it goes. Each day you get a little better at managing your thoughts, the planning starts to take hold and you'll see success in small steps.

Lastly, put the plan into play and start the process through action. This will be both rewarding and difficult. You'll want to celebrate and quit, all in the same moment. Welcome to exercising your mind and thought! Celebrate the successes and move on from the failures; it's the only way you will improve and keep going.

Making Colossal, Long Lasting Changes

A note— in some cases, we're talking about colossal changes of thought. Not just putting a smile on your face and skipping down the sidewalk, but heavy action and a level of patience and persistence you probably haven't experienced. However, there's nothing you can't accomplish. Those aren't just words; it's been proven by people all over the world. Overcoming obstacles is something uniquely human and done by people every day. We read on CNN and other news outlets of the man or woman that loses hundreds of pounds. Just a regular obese person making a change. But do you really think they woke up one day with such a firm resolve to never make a mistake? No. In order to do something that monumental you need to have that desire to change and then resolve to overcome the obstacles that come your way, whether that is sleeping in instead of exercising, eating a piece of cake or overindulging at the buffct. Those challenges will happen, and many may happen for a day, a few days or even a week. Maybe longer? Ultimately, you need to forgive yourself and focus on thought change that leads to sustainable action.

I lived this exact example. I won't dive into all the particulars here, but I'll relay a little bit of my own struggles. I was a skinny kid and graduated high school with a 28-inch waist. I would have loved to be bigger, more muscular and stronger. When I was 20, I finally hit what I wanted. I was happy about it; finally, I filled into the body I wanted. I felt a little like Anthony Michael Hall, the weakling actor of the Breakfast Club who ultimately grew into his own in Edward Scissorhands. I felt good. Then the pendulum shifted, and I started gaining weight. At first it was a little, then more and ultimately, I was a good 140 pounds overweight. Every excuse that could be made, I made. I would go to bed at night with my stomach full, a clear mind and tell myself tomorrow I will have willpower.

Willpower would last long enough for me to eat my second bowl of sugary cereal.

I really didn't look that bad. Then one day I was diagnosed with Type 2 diabetes, which ironically helped guide me to change for a good two months. I would catch a view of myself in the mirror, get a good shock and then change my thought pattern to think of something else. Not the change of thought needed.

What finally got me to change? Well, it's a gradual and continual battle. One I'll need to review and reengage for the rest of my life. What changed is I started to feel my demise, my body slowly shutting down. It scared the crap out of me. I sucked majorly and I knew it. I made a few drastic choices in my life, things that could help me, and I've lost 110 of those 140 pounds. Before you congratulate me, or I pat me on the back, I'm in a constant battle with my thoughts and actions. As I write this, I'm in a battle to eat right and exercise. A real battle and I'm trying to win. Not right now, not today, but I will change my thoughts and lose those last 30 pounds. Right? That's the out I'm giving myself. 110 pounds is great, the 30 extra pounds will come someday when I'm ready.

We control the thoughts, or the thoughts control us, and thoughts lead to action or inaction. I relay this story to you because I'm an active participant in the thought to action to outcome program. We all are, and we all will be.

Final Thoughts on Thoughts

Love the journey, realize that you are going to make mistakes and you resolve to get better. But remember, the objective is to "Suck less", not more or even the same. Don't sugarcoat this and give yourself too many outs. Commit, recommit and find people that can help you do the hard thing and change your thoughts and ultimately your actions.

Consider this poem by Ella Wheeler Wilcox:

"THOUGHTS ARE THINGS"
You can never tell what your thoughts will do
In bringing you hate or love,
For thoughts are things, and their airy wings
Are swift as a carrier dove.

They follow the law of the universe -
Each thing must create its kind -
And they speed o'er the track to bring you back
Whatever went out from your mind.

Our thoughts are things. Each thing creates its kind. Those are poignant lines; our thoughts define us, our thoughts create us, and our thoughts are our future.

If only life was as simple as, "Oh, I get it! Done deal, I am now thinking skinny or happy or whatever and, in a few months, I'm going to be the best me ever!" Don't laugh too hard, we all know someone who finally got their lives to "click" and they are on an unstoppable path. But will it be you, that can be you and that should be you. Or us. Seriously, it should be us. It will be us.

Do I sound a bit like a cheerleader? I hope so, because that is what I want to be for you, your cheerleader. We accomplish nothing in this life on our own, we all need a team. A supportive team, not your family and friends that think they're doing you a favor by holding you back and limiting your expectations. If they're good, have them join the team, and if not, then have them ride the bench.

Tonight, you'll go to bed excited and ready to tackle this. But tomorrow morning, when it's time to get things started with your new and improved thoughts, be prepared to hit the self-limiting belief wall. Expect it. In the next chapter we're jumping in and handing those self-limiting beliefs together.

Pills

1. Write a letter or make a video for yourself when you are truly happy that you can read or watch when you are down and feeling poor. I have this letter, but I also have a video I made for myself when I was totally jacked up and firing on all cylinders that I watch to I remind myself of my greatness and ability. Make one for yourself too.
2. What realistic thoughts can you have? What realistic questions do you need answers to?
3. What colossal, long lasting changes do you need to make? Do a self-inventory. Where can you start that would have the greatest impact on your life?
4. Reread Ella Wheeler Wilcox's poem and internalize it. "Each thing must create its kind," gives you insight into why the thoughts you send out are the thoughts you receive back.

6 HOW IMPORTANT IS "IT" TO YOU?

We all like to feel accomplished; that our day or event was meaningful. Yes, we like downtime where we just do little and decompress from life. Most of all, we want to feel accomplished. But how do we determine whether we've accomplished anything?

Even deeper than the need to feel accomplished is our need for a deep-seated conviction as to what's important. For this purpose, we're talking about the few things that should be driving you forward; those things that dominate your thoughts and cause you pain if you don't work on them.

The Few Dominating Thoughts of Focus

If you were to look at my daily Opportunity Pipeline—not a to do list, but a list of opportunities that I want to accomplish before going to bed you would see three things. Writing this book, exercising and eating well, and the growth of my cybersecurity business. These three things dominate my thoughts. I obsess over them. It hurts me if the day ends and I haven't done well in each one. In writing this book I have a deep feeling that I can help others and help myself along the way. It consumes me, as I write I get the constant nagging thought, "Is what I'm writing compelling and am I relaying my thoughts accurately?" I'm not a writer, never thought about it and then one day I had this burning and overwhelming desire to write this book. It was odd, I'm driving down the road and the thought comes to me that I should write a book on pinpointing focus and having an unceasing resolve to accomplish our dreams and objectives. I went from zero to 60 in a second. Now, I can't stop thinking about it. I write and I feel like I'm on my way to accomplishing the new objective, I don't write, and I realize the lost dream and opportunity for that day. These three things consume me, I wake in the morning and my thoughts immediately turn to what I can do today to accomplish them. When and what am I going to write? Do I have a schedule to exercise? Am I on track to manage my nutritional goals? With my business, what are my prospecting goals for the day? Are we meeting our monthly, quarterly and annual revenue targets? And the thoughts go on and on—and that's just as I wake up in the morning!

Throughout the day these thoughts continue to consume me. I'll ask myself if I'm letting precious time slip away while I'm doing a meaningless task that could be delegated. As an example, in my business recruiting is critical to our ongoing success. The person with the best skills to do this work is me. That's causing disharmony for me because I know that work must get done, I also know that it's an activity that stalls the financial growth of the company. In a given week upwards of half my time can be dedicated to this task, when I need to have clarity on the major growth plan of my company. and half of my time is spent in an area that doesn't do that? In this case I've dedicated thought on how to address this, where it meets the needs of the company as well as me. The solution to this dilemma is that I redirect my time into finding an in-house recruiter to offload most of the tasks and refocus my time back to where I have the greatest impact.

So, you see, discomfort is good, assuming it propels you in the right direction. Otherwise, discomfort is just uncomfortable! It sounds obvious, but it's something we allow all the time, whether it's scarfing down a double bacon cheeseburger with fries and a milkshake or letting ourselves be trapped in a failing business. In my case, the discomfort with how little time I was spending on the company's financial growth built over time to the point that it needed to be resolved.

Reviewing My Tasks, Grading the Day and Planning the Next

At night, the thoughts of what's most important continue to consume me. Have I given sufficient time and energy to each task? Did the objectives set meet expectations? What could I still do this evening to complete unfinished tasks? Like most people, late in the day isn't my best time to be productive. That doesn't mean I'm not productive, just not as much as in the morning. Therefore, it's ideal to get things done early. But life happens; things come up and distractions happen. Anything that takes my focus off my tasks counts as a distraction, so I factor these distractions into my plan. I do this because my wife, children, grandchildren and close friends are all important to me. I set aside time so I can be helpful, loving and meaningful to those most important to me. When it comes to setting time aside for other things, such as family, my tasks now become the distraction. So, whether you are focused on your tasks or on your personal life, make sure to be all in and fully committed.

Before I end the day, I take time to grade myself on how successfully I accomplished each opportunity. I evaluate what went right and wrong, and why. Using my health goals as an example, I look at my caloric and carb intake versus the limits I set for myself. I consider which foods may have been good choices and whether or not I want to add those into my regular routine. Likewise, I review which foods are problem foods. I then plan the next day and what I'm going to eat for breakfast, lunch and dinner with added snacks. This is the simple part; it's following it that's the hard part. I do this with all my tasks for the next day and repeat the process of evaluating them.

Determining Your Key Areas of Focus

So now we've discussed my key focus areas, what are yours? What are you going to do with them? Chances are that you already have an idea on what your few opportunities are, like me they are probably bubbling up and occupying your mind constantly. You may be in tune to those few opportunities or you may not even be aware of what they are, but they are there. If you know what they are you probably have a history of brushing them off and putting other, less important things first. If you don't know what those few opportunities are, you may feel lost or empty. Whichever it is, don't beat yourself up. That's something we do often, we shame ourselves for not sticking to our few opportunities or even not knowing what they are. Don't do it, Instead, focus on action, positive attitude and cutting yourself some slack. In a day and age where we're all expected to be overachievers, we allow ourselves very little wiggle room for mistakes. And, if we are all truly overachievers does that mean we're all normal? Average?

If you fall into the group that doesn't have clarity on your opportunities, don't fret. You are part of the majority. That's not a bad thing; we're just going to need to work together to help you determine your goals. Once we've determined those few opportunities, we can work together to prioritize and develop them until they propel you into success and growth. You'll develop those of greatest importance and purge the ones you find don't measure up as one of your few opportunities.

The Opportunity Pipeline Teaser

By now, I'm sure you've picked up on the fact that I use the term opportunity, rather than task. This is because it is easy to look at something as a task; something you just have to get over and done with. But by training our minds to look at things as opportunities instead we can start to appreciate what is before us, instead of dreading it. We can see them for the value they hold, instead of some meaningless task to push through so we can move onto the next check box. Subsequently, rather than a to do list, it is an opportunity pipeline. By calling it a pipeline, we suggest to our subconscious that we can build an unending stream of opportunities to build upon.

Determining the Niche of Focus

Often you hear people speak about choosing a niche within your business and focusing on that to help your business grow. When I faced this with my company, I looked and said, "Security is our niche." We didn't come out and say that, but that was the message. You need cyber security services? Fantastic, we can help! But we found ourselves chasing deals to meet revenue goals without realizing what that was doing to our business. Getting in financial trouble caused us to analyze what we were offering and dialing in our specific niche. Once we started to do that, we saw our services improve, revenue increase and profitability soar. These changes were what allowed us the opportunity to dig ourselves out of the mess we created.

Too often people try and do too much. They gravitate to many things, instead of doing a few things well. Instead, we should live our life like we're searching out our niche. Do a few things well and master them before moving onto the next. I find three to six opportunities at one time manageable while keeping me focused and engaged. Any less and I get bored, any more and I find myself chasing every shiny object crossing my path. At that point they are no longer opportunities, but distractions.

There is a belief today that we should have multiple streams of income and I completely agree with that. However, I don't always agree with how people get there. Say a millionaire has seven streams of income—people will try and emulate that, starting out with seven streams for themselves. Doing this without building a good opportunity into a great opportunity is what I disagree with. I can't imagine your average millionaire saying, "I'm going to have my seven streams up by the end of the year." However, that's what people do.

Instead, take a business opportunity and nourish it, create it, develop it and have it become something that is sustainable and capable of functioning and living without you. Then, rinse and repeat. It's okay to build your streams slowly. Build your few opportunities around sustainable growth and meaningful achievements. Today my company thrives because we're able to see the future and act on select opportunities, not everything that comes our way. It won't stop all problems, but it allows us to have greater visibility.

Personally, this book will move off the Opportunity Pipeline and it'll be replaced with my next great one. My company will fall into that too. Indeed, as I write this, I'm putting into place new leadership to take that opportunity to the next level. I imagine my health will always be a constant opportunity for me and won't leave my three to six important opportunities.

What opportunities motivate you, get you excited and moving toward your goals? How can you take your existing efforts, rekindle that love, and make them the opportunities they were born to be?

Pills

1. What opportunities should you be obsessing over that deserve your focus and time? How will you make those opportunities a priority in your life?
2. Start planning out your next day's opportunities and how you will achieve a minimum of 80% of the items you have listed. Don't be like the 40% most people get done with a traditional daily to-do list! What could be your niche focus?

7 BURN BABY, BURN

One of the biggest jokes I have with my grown children is my love of soapboxing. If it was an Olympic sport, I'd be a gold medalist many times over, with the culmination of a brilliant career with my image on a Wheaties cereal box, I'm that good. Throughout this book you are going to hear me soapboxing and if we both pay attention, then we may learn a thing or two.

So, without further ado, let the soapboxing begin.

Create a Burning Fire of Desire

Why would you pick up a book and not read it? If we could wager here, I'd take the bet you don't finish this chapter. Let alone read the book. I'm sure somewhere there is a stat that shows how often someone takes something on, only to push it aside and forget about it.

We talk a big game; we make big promises and we collectively fall flat. There are very few people that put action into play and follow it through to its end or its maturation into the next great action. The people that can do this accomplish amazing things, as they've been able to put together a process and follow it. Yes, they make mistakes, but ultimately, they get back to their plan.

Following a plan can be tedious and it's easy to lose that desire. Take NASCAR racing, which I know little about, but the sport is fascinating. Did I just lose credibility? Seriously, NASCAR is fascinating. To the novice, it's a series of left turns for hundreds of miles. Bored yet? Life is like a series of NASCAR left turns. Often life appears repetitive: each day you wake up and you do the same thing over and over. You brush your teeth, shower, put your clothes on, eat breakfast, drink water, etc. I could go on but it's only going to get more repetitive. But repetitive is a good thing! Yes, sometimes you should shake it up and get outside of bad habits, but repetition can be good. Ideally, you make a series of small changes to the repetitive with the occasional shaking things up in a big way to reach new and bigger things.

But what does this all have to do with NASCAR? Well, NASCAR races are won in the seemingly small, but very large details. It's in the pitstop. How quickly can a tire be changed? What about fuel being added? Do you change any of the tires at all and instead hope you have enough tire to get through the final stage of the race? Every detail in the pitstop plays a significant role in the outcome of the race. The crew with the best pitstops often win the races.

For you, the pitstop is the details of your life. Are you taking time to review the items most important to your success, and how often? Are you looking at what can be done this minute or hour or day to impact your future? Or have you checked out and gone back to watching the race from the stands? What things do you need to implement or recommit to right now that will help the rubber meet the road?

Care for Yourself, Follow Your Plan

Here's a bit of ice-cold truth: most people really don't care that much about you. They say they do, but they really don't. Let me tell you a quick story to illustrate my point. In the writing of this book I asked ten people to read a chapter for me. These weren't family members, but people I'm close with, and each should have cared enough to take the time to read it and provide feedback. This was a small ask, but of those ten, one person read it and provided me with feedback. That's it. Yes, people get busy and things come up, but nine of them let me down. And this was a very small thing, it's not like I was asking them to be my getaway driver after a bank heist!

But, with one out of ten people following through that puts me in great company. Jesus Christ himself healed ten people and only one turned around and said thank you. I can't expect more than that! That said, we should all expect and strive for more from ourselves.

You care about you first, build that fire, let it burn and stoke it until it's so hot that people complain. You care about you; few others will care. That's the cold hard truth. Here's the beauty though, care about yourself, build that fire hot and then give embers to others. Just because others don't care about you as much as they should doesn't mean you shouldn't care about them. However, don't count on others to get things done for you, count on yourself. Lean on others where appropriate but realize that when it comes down to it you may hear more excuses as to why the help wasn't there than actually seeing it come to fruition.

Burn It Hot

Why is this important? There are no excuses. Counting on yourself and knowing there are no excuses should be liberating. Knowing that the only obstacles in the way have been put there by you should set your mind free. If you put them there in the first place, then it's much more likely that you'll be the one to remove them and ideally remove them quickly. Even if you choose to leave the obstacle in place it's still your obstacle; you own it. The stronger your fire is and the hotter it burns, the quicker you'll search for ways to remove the barrier and start moving forward again. Let that fire cool, and it becomes much harder to get it going again as you'll be working from a deficit from where you could have been if you never let them cool. Count on yourself, , build your own obstacles, learn to tear your obstacles down quickly, and keep stoking your own fire. Burn baby, burn.

Right now, your fire might be nonexistent, or it might be burning so hot people are starting to complain. If you find yourself sitting around talking about what others are doing or should be doing with their money, or generally complaining about work, family, life or anything in between you have no fire. At best, you might have a pilot light—congratulations! We have something to work with. If you have no fire, then you have lots of company. If you have a fire and it's burning in your gut, then let's point you in a direction where you can start burning things down.

Use Knowledge to Fuel Your Fire

All fires need fuel and, in this case, the more the better. Look around you, where can you get some fuel? Whether you have a physical copy of this book in your hands or are reading the electronic version you have fuel. Books are a great place for fuel, and like any good pyromaniac you need to get your hands on as many as you can.

But let's clarify a few things first. Novels may be entertaining, but they're not fuel. They are fuel suppressants. In April 2016, a Huffington Post article titled, "The Reading Habits of Ultra-Successful People," stated that in a study of 1,200 wealthy people, all had reading as a common pastime. They read to educate, not to be entertain and each was highly selective in what they chose to read. Warren Buffet reads 500 pages a day, Bill Gates 50 books a year and Mark Cuban reads 3 hours a day. No excuses, we all start the day, each day, with the same 24 hours. Those are phenomenal numbers by phenomenal people, however my suggestion is to focus on just a few books and become an expert of that content.

I read whenever I can, both through my Kindle reader and through

Audible. Purists will say listening to an audiobook isn't reading, but they are wrong. What I'm looking for is knowledge. How can I take the knowledge others have and transfer it to me as quickly as possible? I drive a minimum of 45 minutes a day during the week, which means I can get in around 180-200 hours of reading in a year that otherwise might go to useless activities like listening to music, sports radio or (please kill me) politics. That time is a goldmine; it's a vein you can harvest knowledge from over and over.

When reading, find the few books that resonate with you, the ones that can get your head right quickly and can help stoke that fire fast when you most need it. Keep them in your arsenal so you can pull from them when you most need them. There are two or three that I listen to when I need a good kick in the rear. Personally, I like a blended book that provides me with motivation followed by solid action. However, I'm always searching for topics that I feel are areas I need development in; things that can push me up and over obstacles. Right now, I'm researching machine learning and artificial intelligence, what the opportunities are and potential social pitfalls.

Find Others that Are Fueling Their Fire to Help Fuel Yours

Another great way to add fuel to your fire is associate with people that are lifting themselves up and are more than willing to lift you up with them. Find people that are rising up in life and looking for support with their own endeavors. They'll want to help you because it helps them, and in turn you will build up a partnership that moves toward success.

On the flip side, there are many around you, even within the walls of your own home, that who either won't or can't support you; they are detractors and naysayers who generally want to keep you and the world down around them. Don't dump them but move them to an appropriate category in your life. Detractors and naysayers need to be addressed quickly. I have one family member who, regardless of what

I say, always wants to turn it into a fight. So, every time we speak, they get a minute—if they can keep it civil, they get another. Ideally, over time things will normalize, and we can have a meaningful relationship.

Even now, I look for extraordinary relationships; people that can catapult me into greatness, and I them. Those people are out there, you just have to know where to look and how to find them.

Along with associating with good people is the need to find great mentors. Mentors can be people that you know, or those you follow in books or podcasts. My mentors tend to be people I can relate to, have been where I've been, have accomplished great things and have a desire to see others succeed. Do they need to know me personally for that to happen? Absolutely not. One of my mentors died before I ever knew of him, another, as of this writing I'm relegated to fanboy status. Very humbly stated, I would like to be your mentor. Your success, in business, personal, spiritual, health, you name it, is very important to me. There is a caveat, however. You need to step up to the table and perform. You need to commit, to doing, to failing, to brushing yourself off, trying again and preparing to do it repeatedly. I hate quitters.

Step up to the Plate and Be Prepared to Swing

Recently, I was part of a panel discussion on the future hiring and educational need for the cyber security field, an area I have been involved with for over 20 years. The audience was a group of roughly 60 students looking for an insider's edge on what specific niche to focus on, how hiring managers think, importance of industry certifications and many other tidbits they could take away and leverage. I genuinely wanted to help these students out in areas that would benefit them long term and give them leverage over others. When asked what piece of advice I would give them I quickly said, "Build your network." Often, technical people neglect their network, so focus on that as a key area for improvement.

I then offered two ways in which I could personally help them. First, I told them to send me a LinkedIn invite and then ask for an introduction to one of my connections. If their message was compelling, then I would forward it on as a recommendation for them to have a more in-depth discussion. Secondly, if they sent me an email I would sit down with them individually and help them more personally to define their career directions and assist with expanding their presence within the security community. Those were great gifts, ones that each person should have jumped on. But only two people sent me a LinkedIn connection, and only one of them ask to meet. No other person took me up on the offer to meet.

Let me add a bit more flavor to this that may drive this home. I told them I hire people like them and look for talent from the local university. Secondly, I drew a line in the sand and told them that out of 60 people I'd be shocked and immensely impressed if even five of them set up a time to meet with me. Why would I offer so much of my time to these students when I honestly didn't have the time to spare? Because people are their own archenemies. You are your own archenemies. I'm drawing the same line in the sand and saying you don't have it in you to take the steps needed to make the advancements you need for your own success. Sadly, I was confident that numbers would play out and I wouldn't be required to spend that much of my time with them. I ended up being right, but I desperately wish I was wrong.

Invest in Yourself and Commit

This is what I want from you: I want you to prove me wrong. Show me that you aren't your own worst enemy. You need to prove that you can build a fire that burns deeply, that you can do the hard things, and that you can take control of all aspects of your life. Fire fluctuates in its intensity, it's up to the builder of the fire to regulate the heat. In this case as the builder of your own fire you need to get that fire to burn as hot as it possibly can, there is no fire too hot. Just like with real fire building you need to pay attention to it. There will be times where you are in the middle of a time-sensitive project and stopping to add fuel to your fire makes little sense, but that's exactly what you need to do. You need to stoke your fire up and accomplish the project so you can put it behind you and build the big fire again. In NASCAR, when they head to the pitstop close to the end of the race they fuel up just enough to get them to the finish line. Once done I can only assume the driver goes into the needed decompression, only to stoke that fire again. For us, as the driver of our own life, we need to remember to burn it hot.

Burn baby, burn.

Pills

1. What books do you read repeatedly? Are you reading for knowledge? Have a few books you read repeatedly and build up a stable of books to read once you've gained the needed knowledge from the current ones. What books should you add and what knowledge do you currently need?
2. Find places where you can associate with likeminded people. Others that will lift you and not criticize you for a fire burning deep and hot. There are people out there that will understand your obsession, so seek to find those people.
3. On a scale from 1-10, where does your fire burn? Keep it above a seven but push for it to be a constant ten.
4. Who are your mentors? Study them, embrace them, learn and take away those things you find most valuable. Lean on them daily.
5. There are opportunities out there; listen for them and act upon them. The greater your fire the more likely you are to see and act upon those opportunities. If the opportunity doesn't exactly fit your needs, see if you can change it so it does.

8 HOLDING ONTO THE POWER THAT IS YOURS

Gaining or holding power is often looked down on. Growing up, we're taught that we should never seek power. Why is that? We think in terms of, "If I have power someone else doesn't." But that's not the case. You have power that is uniquely yours and you can shrink it, grow it, give it, keep it and mold and shape it in just about every form you can think of. We're talking your power, not others, what you own and manage. But for some reason we don't like applying the word power to this. I'm here to tell you not only is power good, it's glorious. Sweet, sweet power.

The power is yours and it always should be. Never give your power away. Don't let anyone borrow it, have it or use it. It is your power to use and grow. You want as much of it as you can get. The more, the better. You don't give your power to your spouse, your children, your parents, your employer, your peers or anyone. Rise to your power. Rise to your highest level. Are you religious? If so, do you think God gives His power to anyone? Definitely not. He holds all power.

Shying Away from our Power

Why do we shy away from our power? Why does the mere discussion of holding power cause many to flinch? It's easier for us to trick ourselves into an altruistic view that we're above the notion, that somehow being powerful means that we're taking advantage of others. Much of the reason behind our rejection of power has to do with feelings of guilt and inadequacy. However, we can hold onto our power even during times that we feel this way, and we should. In fact, during those times when we are most vulnerable is when we must be our most powerful. A combination of vulnerability and powerlessness often lead to poorer decisions and an ever-decreasing level of hope. Power needs to be held regardless of the emotional situation you face.

This is absolutely critical, and I want to drive this home to you. Again, you cannot, and should not relinquish your power. If you make a mistake, small or colossal, you never give up your power. No one has the right to take that away from you. Power does not mean you are domineering or lack humility. You should always allow people to have their power and to express themselves, even if it's against you. However, that does not mean you should shrink or accept their input.

Dealing with Shrinking Power and Regaining Dignity

Let me give you a few examples of what I mean.

As you know, I had a few rough years. Sales objectives and expectations weren't met, so we hired what we believe to be an industry elite heavy hitter and he tanked. We kept thinking he was just about ready to close the big deals in his pipeline, he repeatedly told us the contract was in procurement to be signed. We kept him around for eighteen months because we knew he was "just about there" and we'd recoup those lost earnings. In the meantime, we took out a short-term loan that we couldn't pay back. Oh, and the IRS wanted their money too. We were left with unmet dreams, debt and back taxes. It felt like we had coals heaped upon us from all angles.

There were times with both the hard money lender and the IRS I gave them my power, especially early on. I felt that since I hadn't paid as I had agreed to, that I was unworthy or unequal to them. I had to accept that they were right, and I was wrong, because I couldn't pay them back. I felt disempowered. As time went on and as I pushed back because we didn't have the money to pay, I slowly regained my power. Toward the end of paying off the debt I had regained all my power. However, in hindsight I realized how much lost time I spent worrying about what they would say and do. There were countless days where I lived in fear, needlessly worrying and giving away my power. I did not need to fear any of them—my fear was a choice.

Regaining and Learning with Power

Regardless of the situation, whether you are in a mess like I was, or you feel you are a victim you do not have to relinquish your power.

To continue with my all too real-life example; like most people I felt bad, I couldn't believe I'd gotten myself into this mess and I felt drained and inadequate. I worried about that phone ringing, about the hard money lender calling me. I know they were about to close my business down any minute or send the police to my door. The IRS was expecting a check from me Tuesday but I am not sure the funds would be in the bank in time, it was something that was keeping me up at night. And so, it goes, I bounced from one worry to the next all the while feeling diminished and inadequate. There went my power. I felt it being taken away from me, my dignity stripped from me and my business and life falling down around me. Here's the thing, no one had taken those things from me. I was choosing to give away my power.

Harnessing the Power Within

If you find yourself in similar situations, then you should feel an immediate flush of confidence with the thought that you are giving it away and it's not being taken from you. That means it's yours. It also means that you can take it back and use that power for your own good and for the good of others. You are kind of like Superman and

Batman all wrapped up into one. Or you know, maybe Wonder Woman and Supergirl?

Imagine this outcome instead. The past few years haven't gone well in my business. I've got lots of debt and I owe the IRS. Our revenue is behind schedule and it's going to take us years to catch up to where we were, let alone where we should be. The IRS wants their money, we have an agreement but it's not going to be easy to stay on top of that monthly payment. The hard money lender isn't so nice, they're ringing our phone with threats every other day. Things are tense, times are uneasy, and I fight a daily emotional rollercoaster. I have made some difficult decisions over the past several months, we let go of an unproductive salesperson and we've spent hours analyzing our financials. It isn't pretty, but it is what it is and that's what we must work with. Whichever way we decide to handle the hard money lender and however the payments to the IRS play out I know a few things. We are going to do what's best for our company, employees and clients. I am going to lead; I am going to handle the hard decisions and I am going to make changes and get things back on track. That's powerful. In this scenario I kept my power, I own it and I'm not giving it to anyone.

You see how these scenarios are the same, but for one key difference? In this one, I keep hold of my power. That's all it takes.

Holding Clarity Through Power

Doing this will give you the clarity you need to make decisions from a point of strength instead of cloudy decisions from a point of weakness. Keeping your power is a constant battle; if you let it go for long periods of time then you may get used to being a victim and allow things to happen to you. You will allow the words people use to diminish you. Likewise, fighting to keep your power will not be easy. As an example, when the hard money lender came at us hard with scare tactics, I felt like I'd been punched in the stomach and then kicked in the teeth. The difference was what I thought after I got up off the ground and brush myself off. Was I going to go away defeated and give away my power or was I going to brush it off and stay strong?

So, you've decided you are going to keep your power and not give it to anyone—now you'll be able fix your business and get it back to growth mode. Along with growing your company, you are about to grow and expand your own power.

Avoiding Power Thieves

One of the most common ways people relinquish their power is through their family and friends. Parents guilt their children, siblings make you feel bad for your success, a spouse could be jealous of the time you spend traveling for work. Friends may guilt you for not hanging out with them, a boss may make you feel bad for not staying and working those extra hours. There are as many ways people can try and take your power as there are people on the planet.

In my case, I grew up with depression era parents. They were all about guarding the nest egg and saving for retirement. In my mother's perfect world, I should have gotten a job with the railroad or the postal service. Those were the two places she always pushed upon me. My parents both worked respectable, but humble jobs; my father was retired military and worked for a penitentiary afterwards, While my mother worked as an assistant director of a childcare center at the local army base. Her words always came with a sense of guilt, easily trying to take my power and force me to conform to her view of things. She was a great mother, but she had a limited view that included trying to take my power. Even at the end of her life she said, "Why do you go to conferences to have other people tell you what to do?" She was looking for control, and without even realizing it, she was looking for my power. Many people that try and take your power have no idea they're even doing it. My assumption is that you do this to other people too, disempowering them so you can get your agenda pushed across. But allowing others to hold their power makes you more powerful in turn.

Using Your Power when You Need It

Your power is a precious and special gift from the Creator. It is a gift others want, but you should never give away. If they can control your power, then they can control you. That power is your own ability to build and create, to decide and to grow. Giving away your power takes those gifts from you. Keeping your power will require you to do things that are painful and unpleasant. It will require you to say no, often, and to push forward when others tell you to sit still. It will require you to believe in yourself, to put yourself first, and to be selfish. In order to serve others, you must first know how to serve yourself.

Right now, if you are going through something that makes you feel vulnerable and disempowered, remember to stay strong and to control your power. The things that have happened to you do not require you to bow down, grovel or relinquish your power. Stay strong.

Pills

1. Where are you currently shying away from your power, or giving it up to someone else? What can you do right now to take that power back?
2. What changes can you make to give you back your dignity and strengthen your power?
3. How can you prepare yourself for the next hard thing that comes at you and challenges your power?
4. What are you going to do on a daily basis that will help you harness your power and lessen the likelihood of relinquishing it?

5. Can you identify your power thieves? How are you going to prevent them from taking your power?

9 LEARNING TO ASK YOURSELF GREAT QUESTIONS

When my middle son was a young child, I would tell his mom that "I don't know" was an acceptable response to "What were you thinking?" He would do some crazy thing that might have been reckless or dangerous and she would get upset, rightfully so. When asked why he did it the response, "I don't know" came back. It seemed logical to me, as I remembered being much the same as a young child myself. A better question from my wife would have been to have asked my son a question that would have elicited a discussion, not a canned response.

Asking Simple Questions

As an adult, not asking ourselves great questions can lead us into murky and troubled waters. When we plow headfirst into an action without first considering all potential risks and rewards, we're doing ourselves a disservice. Asking questions such as, "What could go wrong?" "What's the downside?" "By doing this project, what other opportunities like this could come our way?" can lead to a deeper conversation with yourself and ultimately others.

If we had asked, "What could go wrong?" when we took out that loan and opted not to pay the IRS, then the outcome probably would have been different.

So why is it we don't ask hard questions?

In our case, it was because we thought we had deals coming in that would cover paying back both the IRS and the loan. Except this didn't materialize, and the deals fell through. The questions we should have asked were, what happens if these deals don't come through? How do we repay the loan? How do we make up for missed IRS payments?

Hindsight gives us so much clarity. But in the moment, there are emotional factors which cloud our logic. Often it stems from wanting to relieve the pain we face, as humans we tend to gloss over reality in favor of our emotional attachments. We want something so badly that we're willing to forgo logic for a shady view of reality. That's not to say we shouldn't take risks, but perhaps we should do so with a little more thought. What are we trying to accomplish? In knowing what our desired outcome or purpose is, we can look to understand potential pitfalls more clearly, and we may also see clearer paths towards success.

Asking Unknown Questions

At times, there are questions that should be asked that we don't even know exist. Recently, while speaking with a new business colleague he marveled at all we have overcome. Then he commented, "Man, I wish I knew you when you were going through this, I've helped people who have owed far more than you that are in much worse conditions." Really? That was an option? We were so focused on plodding through and freeing ourselves of debt that we never stopped and asked, "Is there a way out of this that's better and quicker?" Perhaps that had to do with a lack of confidence and power. Clearly, we needed to learn to ask questions even when no apparent question is to be asked.

Questions we may ask could be around areas of revenue generation that aren't in our current offering, such as how do we increase our revenue without making any major changes to our business? Are there others we could partner with that could use our services immediately? Personally, we may ask questions that dive into understanding why certain things happen to us. A friend's son asked me once why all his bosses have been jerks and why they were so hard on him. I suggested he search out to find a common theme between all his bosses. He thought about it for a minute and couldn't think of anything that linked them. Knowing this young man's personality, it was obvious to me he was the common denominator. However, he was unaware that the question needed to be asked or answered.

Getting Down to the Few, Good Questions

Many of us complicate the decision process by asking too many questions, rather than narrowing it down. I find that asking one good question and fully understanding it allows me to build on it and come up with deeper questions that produce better answers. One of my first questions now is simply, why does this need to be done? Or, what is its purpose? If I can start to break this down, then I can often formulate a process that leads to a desired outcome.

This is another important point. Always start with the end in mind and ask what your desired outcome is. If I had looked at the loan from the hard money lender and asked this, the answer wouldn't have been to get the money. It might have been, "I need money to cover payroll and expenses until cash flow picks up." From there I could have determined if that was the desired outcome, or if there was something else. Assuming this was correct, then I could work forward from the beginning, and ask what other outcomes were possible if we chose not to take out a loan.

Seeking Out the Help of Others

For the questions which require deep thought it's best to take the time needed to determine an ideal outcome. Decision fatigue plays into how we answer questions and reach conclusions. This is one reason why it's critical to get input from qualified peers. They can ask the important questions you might not have thought of. Peer groups of qualified individuals are ideal for assisting with this. Properly outline the challenge you are facing, the questions you have and any initial thoughts you might have. Once you've presented the need, let your peers have an open conversation, and be an active listener. Take their feedback, thank them for their assistance and give them some idea as to what you are committed to doing next. But remember, the ultimate decision is yours and you must live with it. Your goal is to make the best decision for you.

Always look for the ideal response—the one that provided the optimum result for the needed objective. In my case, the optimum outcome would not have been to turn to a hard money lender. That decision was driven by a need for a quick resolution to a big problem. but that solution masked the outcome; it provided a few months of relief before the problem surfaced again on a larger scale. We made no attempt to define what our optimum outcome would be. I can with some confidence say that it still would have been painful, but not on the same scale. When we mask important decisions with poor questioning and even poorer answers, the outcome is almost always catastrophic. Each stage in the decision tree either improves the likelihood of success or it degrades it to an abysmal outcome.

Learning to Ask Good Questions, with Small Outcomes

Every day we are faced with an onslaught of questions. They could be as simple as, "Would you like cheese with that burger?" If you are trying to lose weight the ideal answer may seem to be, "No cheese." However, the ideal answer comes from a better question posed earlier—where to eat in the first place.

Many of our important questions are like this. Simple. Unseen. Unaware until it's too late and we have both a full stomach and clarity. Again, hindsight is a beautiful thing. It's through these small questions that we can learn to prepare ourselves to manage the large questions and answers when they come. In the discussion of a peer group, that's something you put in place now, so you have it when you need it. Truth is, you need strong peers now, whether you realize it or not. That peer group allows you to access them when you need them. You don't want to have to pull peers together while managing critical questions and needs. At that point you may find yourself with poor peers, sending you down the negative side of the decision tree. Your goal is to prepare to have great peers around you now, and to learn how to manage small questions well. That way, when the big questions come, you are better prepared to respond properly.

Asking Questions When Need is Immediate

You may be thinking that you have critical tasks that need to be handled now. You don't have the time to spare to pull together a peer group. But first, you have more time than you think, even if the window is closing quickly. Perhaps you could ask, "What happens if I choose to do nothing?" "What happens if I delay?" Often, we force a response because of outside pressures, but that doesn't mean you have to respond. Do your best to analyze the need. One trick I will play on myself is to consider myself as an unaffected or non-emotionally attached observer to my own problem. It's not a peer group, but often when I am able to take a step to the side, I gain clarity.

Perhaps you don't have a peer group, but one or two individuals who can listen clearly and respond appropriately. Normally, these are not family. Family is great, but there are some things they won't or can't tell you. You need as close to unbiased advice as you can get. Speak with those people, either individually or together. Come to them with both the issue and ideas to solve your problem. You may have one idea, or several conflicting options you need to narrow down. You'll want to blend your ideas with theirs. But remember, decisions are ultimately yours to decide and to live with.

Once you've made your decision, go back and ask: "What's the worst that could happen if I go through with this? Can I live with that outcome?"

Concluding Thoughts on Questions

When we made the decision not to pay the hard money lender, we did so after much thought and counsel. Some told us to pay them at all costs, based on their gut instincts and belief that the consequences would be dire. But we didn't. Yes, we were worried and fearful, but we took our decision seriously and created the time we needed to pay them. We asked: "What could the IRS do to our business? What could the hard money lender do to our business? Who would I owe personally if we closed the doors today?" Our questions were logical, and they lead to logical answers. This wasn't a time for emotional questions, and the subsequent emotional answers. That's what got us into this mess!

You can ask great questions too. Take the time to formulate them and get clear and logical answers. Not all questions are as simple as, "Would you like cheese on that?"

Pills

1. How can you get in the habit of getting back to basics and asking simple questions? What simple questions should you be asking?
2. What are your unknown questions, and how can you go about finding them?
3. Which questions can you narrow down that will help you make better decisions?
4. Who can you rely on who has the wisdom and experience to help you ask better questions?

10 A CASE FOR FOCUSING

There are so many ways to get distracted these days, more than any other time in history.

I remember listening to an older gentleman speak once. He said, "When I was a kid, if I wanted to find trouble I had to get on my bike and ride for five miles to find it." Today, you only need access to the internet, a TV or a Smartphone and the distractions flow easily.

One of my employees sent me a message via a Slack channel earlier today.

"Hey, heading over to WinCo to grab some energy drinks and snacks. Need me to pick up anything else?"

"Yeah, canned meat."

"Like Vienna Sausages, chicken in a can, Spam or corned beef?"

"Don't forget pig's feet."

"Yeah, that too."

"What about canned brown bread?"

"Wait…is that a thing? Change canned meat to canned stuff. Get canned stuff. Pick up some canned Whoop Ass."

"How about canned heat?"

So, I sent him an image of the 1970's rock band Canned Heat. Now I'm listening to Canned Heat on Spotify.

It is easy to get distracted and lose our focus. Time is a gift that we need to protect, otherwise we lose it. Schedules get ruined and productivity goes out the door, all because of an inability to focus. I get it—it's fun to follow the trail from canned meat to canned heat, to Spotify and to…what was I doing? But that's the problem, it takes us time to reach a level of productivity. Each time our focus veers we must start again and rebuild momentum from the beginning. What might seem like an innocent ten-minute distraction could lead to an hour behind schedule because we have to completely reset.

However, it's not just time and productivity slipping through our fingers. Losing focus also falls in line with the earlier discussion about being present. Have you ever held a conversation with someone, only to find you are speaking to yourself and the other person has checked out? And have you ever done the same?

What does that say about us? We have an inability to focus on another human and to give them our full attention. What are we saying about the person? We're saying that we don't care enough about them to do the smallest and most important thing in listening to them.

Minimizing the Distractions, Concentrate and Focus

Being unfocused usually means you are distracted by more than just one thing. Fortunately, we've concluded that multitasking doesn't really play out as greater productivity, but as multiple layers of distraction. One minute you are working, the next you are thinking about dinner, then the weekend, then the next fleeting thought to run through your mind, only to cycle back through as you attempt to work again. We lose focus with things that appear to be urgent but could be put off until they can be planned and handled. We allow other's needs, urgent or otherwise, to creep into our day. Start saying no! Your time is yours, even at work. As much as possible you need to help your management prioritize your time. You do have the right to ask to wait until you have a break in what you are doing before you help others. People may guilt you into doing what they want even though they're the time thieves, but remember—your focus is as valuable as your time.

Be Cautious of Busy over Focus

Often, we're a victim of the belief that our busy work is getting us to our goals. We do what makes us feel good, and we put off what is important for what is easy or what is least painful.

The period leading up to my company's troubles was fraught with times of unfocused activities. Revenue was good, but I didn't have the disciplined focus required to manage costs and resources. Once everything cleared and we were settling into managing debt repayment, revenue generation and cash flow we became hyper focused. Becoming aware of all the issues in the company forced us to focus, almost as a penalty. One area that slowed the growth of our company during this time was the amount of focus we had to give to debt repayment, the cash flow shell game and constant discussions with creditors and the IRS. I estimate that nearly half our time was spent focusing on areas that had we paid proper attention to earlier, wouldn't have needed such large amounts of our attention then.

Answer yourself this: do you want to master focus and productivity on your terms or do you want to master it for survival? Hopefully, you answered the former. Good focus starts with a great plan, and a great plan should start with a strong vision of where you are going. Think of vision as your strategic objectives and your plan as the tactical implementation of that vision. Plans need to be distilled down to what can be accomplished each day and monitored on an hourly basis. If you wait to review your plan at the end of each day you may find moments, perhaps even hours, that have been wasted. Setting hourly micro-objectives allows you to monitor your time more closely and to reset as needed. You won't eliminate distractions and fully stay focused, but you can reduce distractions and fine tune your focus.

In order to reach that vision and those strategic objectives, you need to do a daily check on the plan to make sure that those hourly micro-objectives are met. It's easy to miss an hourly check in with yourself—in fact, it's easy to miss several hours back to back and not check in at all. It's the daily review of your vision that keeps the attention where it's needed in the long term. It's what will get your focus back on your plan when you start to drift. It's when we allow these distractions to go unchecked that we find ourselves buried in busy, but unproductive tasks. We need to ask ourselves several times daily, how is my focus? Am I staying on track? Is my focus on my plan helping me reach my vision?

Plan, Review, Check and Restate

I use a planner I created for myself that helps me manage my expectations for the year down to the day. This is my Opportunity Pipeline. It's built so that my objectives and greatest opportunities for the year are at the top. I see these first, before I start to build out my day, right down to the hour. The first thing I look for is a reminder of my bigger yearly vision. I allow myself some flexibility to add a few opportunities a year as they come up, but I never remove an opportunity. If it was well thought out at the start of the year it should be good throughout. On a monthly basis, I create my biggest opportunities which bring me closer to my annual opportunities. I review these and imagine how completing them will bring me closer to my annual opportunities. Next, I set weekly opportunities that will bring me closer to my monthly opportunities. Then, the night before the upcoming workday, I set my daily opportunities and follow that with an outline of what I will be doing on an hourly basis. This process allows me to examine all my opportunities.

A word of caution: you may get frustrated as your hour by hour opportunities outline get blown up. Rest confidently, because they will and you will have to reset your hourly opportunities. Your goal, as best you can, is to use this to eliminate distractions and heighten your focus.

There are other things within my Opportunity Pipeline, including a section I call, "My Present State" This is where I talk about what I will accomplish in the future, as if it has already happened. It's one more step in affirming my future as a current state of reality in the making.

Manage Your Energy to Manage Your Focus

In the midst of our business issues was the problem of my ever-diminishing levels of energy. It came from a lack of sleep and the constant worrying, which tended to feed off each other. Worrying would make it so I couldn't sleep, and I couldn't sleep because I was up worrying. Both caused an increasing inability to focus, because proper sleep and mental health are critical to the mind's ability to fulfil demanding tasks. It's not just that we can't focus, it's that our thoughts are clouded, and we become easily confused. Your brain can't focus without energy, and it needs plenty of it to function properly. When you ignore the brain's need for proper health, you will find yourself tasking your mind with trivial tasks in an attempt to fool it into productivity and focus.

One of many things I learned throughout the ordeal was that I needed to slow down, even when the desire and urgency told me to speed up. The idea of "catching my breath" would initially increase my level of stress, which pushed me back to working harder. I fully believed that I needed to hit the grind like so many people say—and to an extent I still believe this. I've also learned to take a break, to recover. Doing this allow me to accelerate later and have a heightened level of focus.

I found that there are four key areas which allow me to recharge and reset. But when people were demanding their money and I was trying to bail out the company, these things felt like a luxury.

Get Adequate Sleep

Sleep seems obvious, but it's one of the first things we look at cutting even though it's the last thing we should. I won't tell you that you need seven to eight hours of sleep a night, I'll leave that to the experts. Others say you can get by with five or six hours and then have that much more time available to work. I often hear people brag about how early they get up so they can get more done in the day than others, as if waking up early gives them more hours in the day.

That's total rubbish—and that's coming from a guy that considers waking at 5 am sleeping in, with my preferred waking hour at 4 am. The amount of sleep your body needs is unique to you. I now try to fall asleep around the same hour nightly, but I wake at different hours. I also find there are days when I need to sleep in a little later because it's obvious my body needs it. Additionally, I've been known to pull up a couch from time to time at work and take a quick 20-30 minute nap.

What I learned firsthand was that my business needed me energized and focused, and it wasn't going to happen with sleep deprivation setting in. When that happened my concentration was disrupted, cognitive functions slipped and my ability to remember, concentrate and focus all drifted.

Exercising for Increased Focus

As I've mentioned before, my weight was up and my health was slipping. My diet was pretty simple—if it was food, I ate it. My exercise program was equally simple; it was repeatedly walking to the refrigerator. But I learned I could do both simultaneously. I stumbled upon exercise as a great way to release stress, create focus and lose weight. It took all my patience and focus to stay on that elliptical machine early on. I would do twenty minutes, because it was all I could handle physically and mentally. But it doesn't take long for you to get into the groove of exercising. As stress was released, my confidence and my focus all increased. I truly believe in the benefit of energy for focus and focus for energy—they feed off each other and it multiplies.

Meditating for Focus

The third area, and the one I need to work on the most personally, is meditation. It's both frustrating and relaxing for me—frustrating in that I tend to act like a three year old going down for a nap as I'm usually over stimulated and my mind is racing. The first five minutes is a battle to stick with it. But it's relaxing because once I get past those first five minutes I settle in, clear my mind and reap the benefits. Sometimes I even fall asleep!

Meditation provides us with improved concentration and increased mindfulness that often aids in memory recovery. I find that quick, 10-15 minutes of quiet meditation sessions, aided by music or word or just stillness and controlled breathing help to heal and increase energy and focus.

Taking a Break to Regain Focus

Finally, take a break. Just remove yourself from what you are doing. Go to a movie, watch nature, play a game or whatever you need to do just to step back. There are times when I've worked on a project and have given it all my attention and focus, but no matter the sleep, exercise or meditation I do I just need to step away. It doesn't have to be long; just enough to help you reset. I'm often surprised at how refreshed and refocused and motivated I am following a break. Often, during and after a break I experience a spike in creativity.

A final thought. There's a hotel close to our office, and I will go there during the day to have a clarity break. Just me, my mind and my thoughts. I take in the hustle that's going on, the meetings taking place and I just watch. I'm not thinking specifically about anything. I leave my electronic devices at the office or put them on airplane mode. I'm just there to let thoughts form on their own. Often, I come out with great ideas and improved creativity. Sometimes it's just an increase in gratitude.

Then, it's back to the office with renewed energy and focus.

Pills

1. What do you have going on right now that is pulling your focus away from what's really important? What changes could be made to regain long-term focus?
2. Can you detect whether you are busy or focused on the correct opportunities?
3. How can you improve your sleep?
4. Take a break, get out and regain your focus. What short break could you take to regain focus?

11 MINDFULNESS AND BEING PRESENT

I was set to attend a three-day seminar, which focused on self-perspective and individual growth. I had signed up the previous year and my wife and I were looking forward to attending. As things happen, we had to postpone our attendance several times, and we were up against the last possible date before it expired. We either had to pay again or forgo it all together. I had no intention of paying again for what I had previously paid.

The trouble was, it was held three days after everything blew up at the company.

The seminar was held Friday through Sunday. Tuesday and Wednesday leading up to it were dedicated to deep conversations with my internal accountant and the subsequent discussion with my former business partner. Thursday was a meeting with our tax attorney about taking the IRS and our hard money lender seriously. By the time we went to the seminar on Friday morning I was a ball of stress. We were told to turn our phones off. No chance—I had to check my email. The truth was that I didn't have to at all, at least not practically—it was solely an emotional need.

We sat in the seminar from early morning until 5:00 PM. That's when I was able to finally pay attention. The seminar went on until 10:00 PM, and I finally was able to allow a few things to sink in.

Working to Toward a Little Perspective on Presence

The next day gave me perspective on how I had been living versus the need to be present and live in the moment. However, I was only getting glimpses of what that could be like. Normally, I spent Saturday psyching myself up for Monday morning, trapped in a constant battle of worry and fear of what waited for me in the coming week.

So, there we were in this seminar about self-perspective and growth, and I couldn't focus. A moment of concentration would go by and I would quickly find myself thinking about my business partner, the IRS, the hard money lender, employees, cash flow, other debt, sales, revenue, etc. I was spinning myself up and down repeatedly. Saturday turned out to be a combination of insight and being fraught with worry of the coming week.

By Sunday I couldn't sit still. Nearly everyone was having life changing epiphanies and I wasn't even close. I was pissed off. What the hell? What was wrong with these people? I felt like I was at a campfire holding hands singing folk songs. I wanted to rip off arms and slap people. That's harsh, but I was a day away from Monday and I needed something, anything to make this worth it.

Hours and hours went by and nothing. The seminar was reaching its end, and after seeing one too many people get what was going on, I was growing increasingly desperate and restless.

I held up my hand. Ignored. I held up my hand higher. Still, ignored. Finally, I stood up with my hand held high, and the instructor called on me. It was about damn time. She calls me up to the front of the room.

"I don't get it."

"What don't you get?"

"Everyone in here is having a moment and I'm sitting back there not having one. What you don't understand is I need this moment. I have some serious issues going on at work that have been brewing over this weekend. I have no resolve and tomorrow this will all be a memory and I'll be back dealing with all this emotional and heavy crap. I need something, seriously, I desperately need whatever these people have."

I can't remember much of what transpired between my plea and her finally getting through to me. However, it ended with something like this.

"Tab, right now everything is okay. Everything is alright."

"Yeah, I've heard you say that to others. But it's not okay or alright. It's a damn mess."

"Tab, right now everything is okay. Everything is alright."

"Still not getting it," I said, as I wished I hadn't gotten up and that I could just leave.

"Tab, you need to understand, that as you are standing there none of those things are real. They are in the future. Right now, as you stand there, you are okay. Wherever you are, you can be okay in the moment. Life is fine just where you are."

For whatever reason it finally hit me, either because I was fighting it or because I was dense. I started to sob uncontrollably. For the first time in a long time I felt peaceful.

Learning to Live with Peace and Prepare to Battle When Needed

I tried to apply what she told me the following day as I drove to a meeting with my attorney and soon to be former business partner. Feelings of anxiety started to flare up and I said to myself, "Right now in this moment everything is fine. There is nothing wrong." As a person who tends to motor at a high speed this was a bit difficult for me. However, I couldn't deny the power of being present.

There's a lot to the subject of being present, but I tend to twist and bend things to meet my personal needs or agenda. When you have cascading troubles, they tend to blend into one colossal hairball. It's just all there, all the time. When we make our troubles into a single trouble we never get to rest—and more importantly, we miss out on the opportunities that are before us, whether that's a business opportunity or a chance to relax with your family.

Living in the present works in all areas of life, not just the good. The seminar was about being at peace and happy in the moment, but I left with another view. When I wasn't dealing with an issue I lived in the present and I felt peace. Likewise, I learned to be present and ready for war when there was an issue. I was willing to battle because I had allowed myself time to rest. I saw this issue as being present for a short duration. Then, when it was over, peace in the moment could happen once again.

Living in the present means taking all the present as it is; not looking at the present solely as peaceful. We can be both present and peaceful and fully aware that things can change in an instant. We also know that at any given time we'll need to go to war. We can live in peace while we prepare for war up until the moment of battle, even if it's just mentally. Often, we spend more time worrying about the battle than we actually spend during it, so we're already exhausted when we head into it. When we learn to compartmentalize events, we learn to rest and have peace for longer stretches.

Living in the present isn't equal to a faucet you turn on or off as needed, it's more of a faucet you leave on all the time. The present just is.

Calling the Present a War

Calling the consideration of managing hard issues war may seem counterintuitive to living in the present. It's not. It's about moving towards having complete awareness of your life. A key advantage of this is leaving worry behind you and focusing on the present. Present living doesn't mean you are oblivious to a future, but that you'll plan where needed and live in the given moment. You are always fully appreciative, even in moments of war. You do this by seeing the battle solely in its moment, rather than allowing it to bleed out into worrying about the future or forgetting the past. Give all your energy to solving the issue in that moment. Going into battle well-rested lessens decision fatigue and bad decisions. It may seem odd to say there is joy in war, but there certainly is joy living in the present, as it allows us to live with energy and awareness. How can that be bad?

I previously discussed a period that I spent sitting in a chair for weeks, overcome with worry, fear and dread. The amount of actual time I took to handle the extremely difficult issues paled in comparison to the time I spent living, reliving, creating nightmares and playing out my imminent doom in my mind. Living in the present would have allowed me to be aware, to see my beautiful wife and live my beautiful life. Instead, I chose not to see her and instead picked the mental anguish of simultaneously living a past and future life of dread. Sound silly? That's because it is. And yet, most of us do that daily.

Love Your Present

Decide now to love what you are doing and where you are at. That doesn't mean you have to love your job or love everything about your life, but that you need to allow yourself to be happy with where you are right now. Consider the good and prepare to handle the battles, and always live in the present, good or bad.

If you are up for it count the hours in a week that you spend living in the past or worrying about your future. UK healthcare provider Benenden Health estimates that the average adult loses roughly two hours a day worrying about their personal finances, job security, health, love life and getting old. All the while they are getting older and worrying about getting older. We spend more than five years of our lives worrying.

There are other time wasters too! We spend time dreaming and dwelling on the amazing past accomplishments we've had or being angry about situations or people that have wronged us. There are many ways we focus on both past and future unhealthily, all the while forgoing the present moment. The present is beautiful, it's reality, and it's happening right now.

Forgiving Our Past, Living a Fortunate Life

Living in the present means we need to forgive the past. We must forgive both ourselves others.

Michel de Montaigne stated: "My life has been filled with terrible misfortune; most of which never happened." There's a study that shows just how accurate Montaigne's comment was. The study considered the distress we feel versus the realization of those things which caused it. Participants within the study were asked to track what caused the worry over a period, and to identify which worries actually materialized. Unsurprisingly, 85% of what participants worried about never transpired.

So, what happened with that 15% that did come to fruition? 79% of the participants learned that they were either able to handle the issue better than expected, or they learned a valuable lesson from the experience. That means that the vast majority of our worries don't add anything to our lives. It's just our thoughts running wild, punishing us with everything they can conjure up and exaggerate.

I can hear some people now saying that the small chance could be what does them in, and if they don't worry it will bring tremendous trouble. But all this worrying about worrying leads us nowhere. Most of our worries are just recycled and repurposed. Step back and look at your life. Put your hand on your chest. Feel that? Its air moving into your lungs. It means you are alive, and you have lived to overcome every worry placed before you. Perhaps you've overcome well, perhaps not. But you have overcome every single one. Congratulations, you are a survivor! Now, stop worrying.

The Future is Beautiful, The Present More So

The past is in the past, but the future lies before us. Dream big, and plan bigger. Consider the possibilities. Take time to meditate and contemplate the future and visualize it as if it is already happening. There is tremendous power in this.

My children had a piggy bank growing up that was Darth Vader from Star Wars; they would put in a coin or push the button and he would say, "Impressive, most impressive, but you are not quite a Jedi yet," (*Star Wars Episode IV: A New Hope*, 1977) and it would fade to the Imperial March. Basically, "Hey, great job! Now, get back to work!" That's the message—get to work. Visualize your future, see what it will be, and get to work to make it happen.

Fully appreciate the moments you have today. Live in the present and, like the instructor at that seminar repeated to me until it sunk in, "Tab, right now everything is okay. Everything is alright." Don't expect to understand this without repeated practice and trial and error. Living in the present takes practice and patience. You must stick with it. Why? Because, wherever you go, there you are. You'll never get away from your present, so learn to love and live in the moment.

Pills

1. What war are you fighting that you can leave alone until it's time to go to battle? What can you do to have peace in the midst of a war?

2. When you are faced with uncontrolled worry, stop and say, "Right now, everything is okay." Can you find your inner peace when peace is normally fleeting?

3. What can you do to forgive yourself and not live with remorse and regrets?

4. Take a few minutes and contemplate just how beautiful the present moment is. Look around you! Find things that are beautiful and state their beauty to yourself.

12 DEFAULT MOOD: IMPENDING DOOM

I would like to think of my spirit animal as the grizzly bear. Big, ferocious, intimidating and prone to long naps with a full belly. In fact, I may be more like the Coues Whitetail deer. Neurotic, fearful, hyperaware and a survivalist. Often called the Grey Ghost, it stands about 32-34 inches and rarely weighs more than 100 pounds. Because of their small stature they're a common prey of mountain lions, bobcats, coyotes, eagles and other animals. The Grey Ghost is a neurotic creature and tends to be in a permanent state of survival, rarely letting its guard down. Dedicated hunters purchase high powered binoculars to scope them out from a distance because it's extremely difficult to get close. All the Grey Ghost needs to hear, or see, is anything that sounds like a threat and they're gone. Hunters say that all they have to do is look away for a second and they've lost sight of the deer, never to be seen again.

While battling for my business's survival, the characteristics of the Grey Ghost were admirable and helped keep the company alive. I was constantly aware of the need for us to drive revenue, drive revenue and drive revenue some more. It was a bit like the deer out in the field needing to eat grass so they would have the energy needed to run like hell with a nanosecond's notice. Drive more revenue, have more money, pay those debts. For years those characteristics served me well. But we would spend more time scoping out the landscape of creditors and when they needed money than we should have, when we should have been driving revenue. However, that's what kept us alive.

Years of living a certain way tend to force us into ingrained patterns of habit; ones that may have served us in the past but no longer do so. The subconscious mind has learned a new pattern, one that has become familiar to us and but can be counter intuitive to our needs.

Self-Awareness of My Impending Doom

One Sunday morning, I was in line to board a plane some time ago with my wife. She had a conference to attend and I was along for the ride. We were looking at a five-hour flight from Seattle to Washington DC, and I had a sinking feeling in my gut. I looked over at my wife and started to go over what has become an all too common discussion.

"Man, something is wrong. I should be happy and I'm not, I have this feeling like something is wrong or something is going to happen," I said.

"What's wrong? Do you have an issue with a client, employee or some other thing weighing you down? Maybe cashflow to make payroll?"

"No, nothing like that, we're doing really well in those areas. But something's not right and I can't figure it out."

That conversation was one that we'd had many times since the company has come out of its troubles.

The Realization of Impending Doom

Finally, and for some unknown reason, but like a gift from God a thought comes, I lived in a world of impending doom!

And at that moment, I was filled with overwhelming joy. After months , perhaps a year, I was able to finally label this unwanted emotion. I could recognize it, state it, address it and manage it. More than that, I could own it! No longer did I need to hide like the Grey Ghost, fearful of what might be out there. And as each day passed, what I feared did not become real. The hardest days—the days with the money lender breathing down my neck—were past me. But the emotions still lingered.

As an aside, I would like to note that the feeling of impending doom can be a recognized medical symptom of anxiety and even heart attacks. Though I am not a doctor, having been in this position I strongly recommend that if you are struggling with this you seek medical advice and follow your doctor's guidance. Perhaps something I say here will help you, but don't replace what I say with good solid medical advice.

In an ideal world, we would be able to find a magic switch that turns that sense of impending doom into believing the sky is the limit. But that's not the case, and as with anything worthy of deep and lasting change, we should never expect an easy switch. Change comes slowly, but ultimately brings about a deeply engrained good habit; the antithesis of the subconsciously driven and deeply negative mood of impending doom.

instead of a light switch, what I was able to find was a road map to replace my negative thoughts. To varying degrees of success, and often depending on the situation, I've learned to self-talk my way out what was a maze of unending thoughts, all of which led to a dead end of doom.

Is the Threat Real?

My initial question now is this: is this impending doom a real threat that needs to be addressed? Normally, the realization is simple, even if the answer doesn't come easily. Emotionally, I may say it is a real threat, but I can't place what the threat actually is. In this case, the emotion that needs to be addressed, not the mythical threat. What I've also learned is that real threats arrive as a threat, front and center in all their glory, not disguised as a bad feeling. You tend to address real threats in real time. You don't sit around wondering—it's obvious when they're real.

When you've learned to live the lifestyle of the Grey Ghost you recognize all threats as equal threats. Mountain lion on the horizon? Run like hell. Wind gusts up? Run like hell. Living the life of the Grey Ghost means that you treat a major, massive threat the same as a minor inconvenience. Both provide equal reason to panic.

Your Gut Can Guide You

Going back to that moment at the airport—I've learned that what I was experiencing wasn't imaginary. Whether the perceived threat is a real or emotional one, my gut takes it as real. In this way, it is all real, which is pretty scary.

That gut feeling comes from the Solar Plexus, which takes the energy we provide and distributes it. Whether the energy is negative or positive, it accepts it as real and works from that view. That's why at one moment you feel hopeless and then a little while later you feel great. This is perhaps not the only reason, but when it comes to the Solar Plexus your shift in thought is a shift in energy and output.

When the Solar Plexus is not operating properly, we are in discord; we can feel it and so can those around us. That discord makes us mentally, physically and spiritually ill. Think in terms of when you are feeling mentally tapped out or physically exhausted from stress or spiritually feeling imbalanced. . We're not talking about severe mental, physical or spiritual illnesses, though that could be the case as well. We're speaking of illness that causes us to become sluggish, be it physically or mentally. Think of it as energy we're feeding our mind and body. If it was fast food versus healthy choices it would resonate easily for us. This is the same; healthy thoughts and energy helps us to function properly, both emotionally and physically.

Here's a bold statement: the Solar Plexus controls all of us. Or, more accurately, the thoughts we feed it controls us. What we feed it causes us harmony or disharmony. The conscious mind is the source of all energy into the Solar Plexus, and from there we get results based off the energy we feed into it. The subconscious mind sees energy as truth; therefore, it sets out to make the thoughts we have a reality based on the information it receives from the conscious mind. If we feed it positive, aspirational thoughts, then our subconscious will help us make them a reality—and so, we can accomplish whatever we set out to accomplish.

What We Think Becomes Our Reality

If that doesn't scare you, then this isn't sinking in. Have you ever felt that you can accomplish a certain task with zero doubt, only to find yourself doubting the same task later even though nothing has changed?

But something has changed—your conscious belief. You went from a feeling of certainty to one of doubt. Through the Solar Plexus the subconscious takes that information as accurate. It doesn't wonder why things have changed. All it does is take the information we provide it as truth, whatever the perception of truth is at that moment.

This means that our thoughts truly are things, or our thoughts are reality. For me, that's either scary information—or it's enlightening and full of possibilities. Really, it depends on how I present that information to my Solar Plexus. I purposely didn't say scary or enlightening in the above paragraph because I wanted to take you down a singular path to a decision; the decision of doom. Thus, we need to constantly and consciously be watchful of the information we allow to enter the Solar Plexus.

Now that you know that there are no limitations to what our subconscious mind will believe, what are you going to tell it? And you will tell it something—actually, you will tell it something thousands of times a day, which means it will believe you thousands of times a day. Most of the time we are completely unaware of what we're telling ourselves.

This is extremely exciting and life changing once we put it into practice. That gut feeling of impending doom? That can be our warning sign to change our thoughts from negative to positive. Instead of saying something doesn't feel right and leaving it at that, use it as a warning to change our thought. Say you need to change your thoughts from negative and scarcity to ones of positive and abundance instead. Too simple? Well, in a world of complexity, simple is good.

It's that simple because we say it's that simple. The Solar Plexus takes the information we give it, and the subconscious assumes truth. If we say it's more complex than that we're correct, it is more complex than that. If we say it's as easy as that, then it's the truth too. Whichever we choose, the subconscious is going to take it as truth. Again, depending on where you are with this, it's either very scary or very exciting. I choose exciting!

Who knew the gospel song by Harry Dixon Loes, "This Little Light of Mine" was so powerful?

This little light of mine, I'm gonna let it shine
Every day, every day, every day, every way
Gonna let my little light shine
Light that shines is the light of love
Hides the darkness from above
Shines on me and it shines on you
Shows you what the power of love can do
Shine my light both bright and clear
Shine my light both far and near
In every dark corner that I find

Let my little light shine

We must let our light shine. The more positive energy we radiate, the more positive outcomes we receive. We can turn undesirable situations into sources of pleasure, and we can remove negative thoughts and outcomes from our lives. We can literally change our world view and reality with the energy the conscious mind creates and delivers to the subconscious.

The opportunity is there for us to radiate energy. Like an oven we can determine the heat we radiate; we can turn it up and burn it down. We can attract people to us through that radiation, and that energy can heal and help people with troubled minds without the spoken word. That energy can heal us. When the Solar Plexus is operating properly, all we come into contact with have the opportunity for a pleasant experience.

Impending BOOM!

My conscious mind now gets excited when it feels impending doom coming, because I recognize that it is showing me the need for immediate change from impending doom to Impending BOOM! So, on that day, as I stood there with my wife, I said, "Man, something is wrong. I should be happy and I'm not, that means there's an opportunity for me to feed my subconscious mind new information. My subconscious mind is gullible, I love it, it believes everything I tell it!"

There is an old adage that knowledge is access to power, and that's true. However, thought is the access to massive power, creativity and delivery of those things we want. Not just any thought, but positive energy based thought our conscious sends to the Solar Plexus. We can create anything.

My hope for you is that you will dive into this, study, learn and practice. Your thoughts can change your reality.

Pills

1. Can you recognize feelings of uncertainty, doubt or impending doom coming over you? How will you address it? How will you reverse this?

2. When you feel a threat coming on, can you stop and ask if the threat is real? How can you determine a real threat versus a perceived one?

3. Your gut, your solar plexus speaks to you. Can you take time to identify what it's saying?

4. Your reality can change depending on your current thoughts. What changes can you implement that will lead to an increased positive reality?

13 EMBRACING AFFIRMACATIONS

It's often recommended that people repeat affirmations to motivate themselves. The concept sounds great; say things which bring you into the mindset you need to rise to the challenges you'll face. But I've always struggled with this idea.

Part of this puzzlement comes from sayings such as, "I am the architect of my life, I create the foundation and I am full of joy, love and peace or I am full of the qualities I need to be extremely successful." For me that just rings hollow. Affirmations need to be tied to something bigger, and more specifically, to your goals. It's my belief that solely repeating affirmations like these may help with your emotional support, but they're not going to make you achieve anything. Your affirmations need to be drilled into your subconscious, and they need to be believable. The more you believe in what you are telling yourself, the more others will get behind your story and help you reach your goals.

The Drill of Cadences

When I was in the military, cadences were drilled into me during basic training. I quickly became sick of it. Although it's been 34 years since I left basic training, I can still vividly remember the cadences. "I want to be an airborne ranger; I want to live a life of danger" rang through my head for years as I ran. I couldn't get it out of there. The cadence we marched everywhere to was, "Yo left, yo left, yo left, right, left" rang out for well over a decade. Each time I had someone walking in front of me I would situate my step with theirs to be in lockstep and then I'd start saying in my head, "Yo left, yo left, yo left, right, left." I couldn't get it out of there; it just happened.

What's amazing is that a drill sergeant could get us all to do these things and believe in them years later. I'm confident that the world is full of people just like me that do these things, lockstep and in cadence essentially collectively alone. Each one of us got behind the goal of the country; regardless of how we felt their story became ours and we worked in unison to help them reach their goals.

Living a Life of Normalcy

I don't want to downplay the need to get yourself to the level where you can make real changes in your life. During my years of business troubles, I certainly could have used some belief in myself; some affirmations to give myself much needed encouragement. Sometimes, reaching a level of being a badass means you first must reach a level of lifting your head up and gaining a glimmer of hope. We just need to do that and move ourselves forward as quickly as possible.

I see most things in life in a series of threes, sort of like a life pendulum. The point is to swing from one end to the other as quickly as possible—but unlike a pendulum, you stay on the productive side permanently. On one side you have negativity, the other positivity and in the middle, you have a state of transition. It's that state of transition that can be the most dangerous to you. The middle is comfortable, its easy and it's where most of society lives, which makes it familiar. It's where we can settle for a very long time, if we aren't careful. In the case of our mindset, it's where we complain about others, but never make a change to our own lives. This is a state of coasting, of complacency, and we don't want that. Instead, let's defy gravity and get the pendulum to shift to the right side!

Taking Affirmations and Making Them Useful

You know what would be better than affirmations? Putting together your affirmations with action—creating what I call affirm-actions. This gives you a positive mental direction that's backed up by action. With affirmation alone you may start the day off with positive thoughts that give you emotional support, but with Affirmactions you remind yourself with affirmation, and reflect with action. It's that action which provides you with a sense of accomplishment and belief. That's powerful. Affirmaction will help you drive home your ideals and goals to teach your subconscious. It's Affirmaction that the drill sergeants used to get us all in lockstep.

What I learned from my time in basic training was so valuable that I've worked it into my life, sometimes to the point of becoming sick of it. However, I do it because it works, and because my subconscious can take over.

My personal cadence is pretty simple; it starts with the word 'these'. As in, "These steps or these reps or these calls or these meetings or these whatever." I repeat this, over and over. For exercise when I'm out for a walk I will say to myself, "these steps, these steps, these steps" as each foot hits the ground. Then I move into further cadences such as, "These steps lead to the next step, these steps lead to the next steps, these steps lead to the next step." "The next step is me lifting weights, becoming big, strong and muscular, the next step is me lifting weights, becoming big, strong and muscular, the next step is me lifting weights, becoming big, strong and muscular."

I say these in my head to I drive home to myself that I'm a badass. I'm building momentum and becoming formidable. I'm becoming a 55-year-old badass who people will see as formidable or they won't.

But if they don't, they'll get hit like a truck—because a truck is coming after them. They can either get with me or get in front of me and get hit. Of course, this is total bravado. The point isn't to run out and do harm to others or to act egotistical or narcissistic. This is about us saying more than positive affirmations; it's about us being positively self-energized to psych ourselves up, get our juices flowing and motivate ourselves. We're jacked up, we're fired up and we're ready to go. We are taking action.

The Spread of Affirmactions

Affirmaction spreads; it can't be contained. Once you turn it on and deliver cadences on your health saying, "These steps", you build momentum into "These steps, lead to the next step." But when you've completed your workout you are not done. Once that fire has been lit, you are onto, "These calls", in our example of the salesperson. It becomes increasingly difficult to slow the momentum as it travels from one part of your life to the next.

As you do this Affirmaction will take place as you go to bed at night—you'll be doing cadences as you drift off to sleep! Chances are, you'll be dreaming in cadence and all the possibilities you could accomplish. When you wake, you'll have a better chance at hitting the ground with Affirmaction to start a new day.

I am very careful as to where I allow my mind to go. I'm looking to affirm what I do, supported by action. Not only do I want to think it, I want to physically feel it. The need for Affirmaction gives me confidence. I want to see myself as I am in the future, not as I am today. I want to be that highly active, muscular and strong badass I am talking about. I need to believe that I am him today and talk with positive affirmation alone isn't going to accomplish that. I need Affirmaction.

Living a Life of Affirmaction

We can act with Affirmaction in all areas of our life. If you are in sales, each time you pick up the phone to make a cold call you can say, "These calls" and build from there. If you are a homemaker, you could say "These floors" and build from there. That's meant to be funny, but that's part of the key to all of this. Love what you do and love the process of what you are doing and becoming. Get out there and put action to your affirmations repeatedly.

Like the military had us all in unison lockstep, you can have others believe in your goals and dreams too. It may be many, or it may be one, but others believing in and helping you reach your efforts and goals will catapult your pendulum. Just the other day I told someone about my epiphany, the use of the word Affirmaction and how I integrated it into my personal daily, weekly, and monthly personal life planner. They jumped on board immediately, suggesting trademarking the term and asking for a copy of my planner so they could use it too. One down, many to go.

But why does that matter? Because effort, knowledge and action all flow where the energy comes from. Ideas rush to us and we start to see that we're onto something as others get behind us. It's exhilarating and it's contagious.

Be on the Lookout for Affirmaction Suckers

Be on the lookout for things that will attempt to take you out of your game; those things that will get that pendulum to swing the other way. They will come at you daily, some of them small and some of them massive. Your objective is to get past them while incurring as little harm as possible. There are a few ways to do this.

Firstly, don't allow negative thoughts to enter your head. Who cares if today you couldn't workout as hard as you would have liked? Who cares if you make a sales call and it went badly? Or who cares if that nicely cleaned floor just had crap spilled all over it? Yes, these things are all bothersome, but don't let them distract you. If you allow these things to fester, then the negative impact will only grow. For instance, on one occasion I lied to a client—I led them to believe that we could do something but didn't follow through before the deadline. My own laziness turned a promise into a lie. I hate doing that; I'm normally so much better than it. I dreamed about this mistake, various scenarios over and over again—some of them made sense, and others were absolutely crazy. When I woke, I continued to feel anxious about it, my stomach tied in knots—after all, I had just created a number of ways I could have handled it better.

You see what I'm doing, don't you? I'm beating myself up and I'm questioning myself. I'm moving that pendulum to the wrong side, and now I must use energy to move it back that I could have used to sustain momentum instead. Do you also see how my subconscious played a part in this? The subconscious never sleeps, whereas the conscious mind does. We need to constantly feed our subconscious mind with positive information. Otherwise, it will work with the negative information the conscious mind feeds it.

It is best to give your subconscious plain and simple tasks, especially at night when the conscious mind is asleep. This is an enormous source of power. In the above example, I fed the subconscious mind crap to work with and it spewed out more crap throughout the night. Your desire and action should be to feed your brain with solid, positive information before sleep. The subconscious mind never sleeps, and so for roughly a third of your life it does as it pleases. That should scare us, but it can also enlighten us to the possibilities.

Our Subconscious can Solve Our Problems

If we fully understood how much our life is impacted by our perception of perfection and our emotions, then we'd handle life with more care. We would have our conscious mind guard our subconscious mind better.

The subconscious mind has the ability, given enough time, to solve our problems. Literally, we could be in a situation where we perceive differences with another person, but when we start to communicate, we find those troubles disappear because the subconscious has solved it. If we trust the subconscious, we find that we have infinite resources at our command. However, those resources need us to feed the subconscious good information so it can access and deliver the outcomes we need. That's both scary and exciting.

The conscious mind must determine and deliver proper information to the subconscious mind, otherwise the subconscious will see false information as truth and deliver the wrong outcome. This leads to second guessing ourselves. If something like this could happen once, could it happen again? When will it happen again? We get wound up as the subconscious mind deals with false information. It's up to my conscious mind to get my subconscious in lockstep and back to doing what it's great at—being instinctive.

The conscious mind is now in damage control. It must tell my subconscious something that makes logical sense. An example of this would be, "Yes, I screwed this up. Life isn't meant to be lived in perfection. Here's the thing, we both want more, lots more than what we have today. That means we push harder, and we get the chance to do more great things. And that's freaking awesome, we want to do more great things! That also means that the more we do, the greater the likelihood we're going to make a mistake. Every time I send you bad information, especially on something big, it's going to stop you and you are going to start questioning us again. That cycle is going to start up all over again."

The objective in this self-discussion is to correct the mindset as quickly as possible. We need to get that pendulum shifting to the positive, and fast.

So, get in there and drive forwards. Make mistakes, do great things, and keep the affirmation and action going. When you do have a set back, get the pendulum to shift back quickly. Don't stop, and don't allow your subconscious mind too much time to dwell on the perils you've put it in. Let the conscious mind guide you back to where you need to be. Keep that fire and action burning.

Pills

1. What Affirmactions can you create for yourself that will both provide you motivation and push you to action?
2. What Affirmaction can you give your subconscious mind to work on while it sleeps? Remember, your conscious sleeps, your unconscious doesn't. What good opportunity can you give it to work on?
3. What Affirmation suckers are living within your life that you need to remove? How and when will you remove them?
4. What cadences were built into your subconscious? What useful cadences can you build into your subconscious?

14 INTRODUCTION TO THE OPPORTUNITY PIPELINE

Day planners, to-do lists and various other methods are all ways to manage our time better. Years ago, back in the dark days of the 80's and 90's, I used handwritten management of my daily calendar and tasks. It all seemed simple and manageable. Now, here we are in 2020 and everyone has the latest and greatest way to manage your time, goals, personal resources, etc. Personally, I've tried many of them out in the search for an edge. I even went so far to take what I saw was the best of three different systems and blended them.

Ultimately, however, I realized that I was still falling short of what I wanted to accomplish. Instead of feeling in control I started to feel rushed to get ahead of things, not just to manage them. Phrases like, critical tasks, to-do lists, schedule of events, daily needs and more left me feeling more like I was chasing a checkbox than I was seeking a great accomplishment.

After driving into the office one day and talking to my wife about the list of critical tasks I had to accomplish I realized I hated those words. I hated how they made me feel. They felt so hollow, and I felt like I was just a hamster on a wheel. In that moment I had clarity. What I needed were actions that aligned with what I most want to accomplish in life.

Instead of a planner or to-do list, I wanted an Opportunity Pipeline. But what's the difference? Part of it has to do with the need to align all I do, from the hourly to the visionary, which includes what I measure daily, weekly, monthly and yearly. But it's also about how it makes me feel. When I talk about critical tasks I feel like that hamster on a wheel. When I talk about the Opportunity Pipeline, I feel possibilities and alignment with all the opportunities in my path.

The Opportunity Pipeline Creation

As with most ideas, the Opportunity Pipeline morphed from simply calling my to-do list an Opportunity Pipeline to a detailed, guided process to increase the likelihood of success. The flow of the Opportunity Pipeline matters, and when used properly it guides you from your "Present State" down to what you need to do on an hourly basis to accomplish your opportunities. If interested, you can download a copy at www.tabpierce.com.

Once downloaded you can follow along and fill yours out as you go along, otherwise this will give you a detailed look at what you can do to improve the way you manage your goals and time.

My Present State

Call this a nod to traditional vision boards. "My Present State" is where I put down my loftier ideas or visions, the ones that I would like to have but don't fit within a specific timeline. That's the key here, I may see them out in two years or beyond, but for the most part I don't have a completion date associated with them. To get your own vision and juices flowing, some examples of things you might consider putting here are:

- My business has a revenue of $10,000,000 annually, of which I make $1,000,000
- I have $10,000,000 in cash and investments
- I own 1,000 apartment units
- My wife and I own a home valued near $3,000,000

This is your playground to add in your own vision and dreams. Personally, I prefer this area filled with items that are a stretch to reach, but not such a stretch that my conscious mind doesn't buy into it, thus relaying a defeated attitude to the subconscious. I can always increase My Present State as my own beliefs and accomplishments grow!

Current Year Opportunities

This is where the Opportunity Pipeline starts to get measurable with dates. Ideally, they track and bring you closer to the visions you created in the My Present State section of the Opportunity Pipeline. This is where you set your yearly goals and opportunities. They're not only attainable within the year, but if tracked well you'll either succeed or even overachieve and surpass your opportunity objectives. Like the My Present State section, you want to make these goals stretch so you can reach them, but not without taking pinpointed actions to achieve each. Assuming the previous opportunities in the My Present State section were what you chose your opportunities, here could be:

- My business has revenue of $3,000,000 annually, of which I make $250,000
- I have $250,000 in cash and investments
- My wife and I have saved $100,000 this year
- Our credit score is 740 or higher
- We have zero debt

These opportunities should excite you each time you look at them. and you should be able to see a path to reaching them. If you've never made $100,000 in a year and you put that down as your money saved, you may not believe that it will happen. You'll probably become quickly disenchanted with this section of your Opportunity Pipeline. This is the one section you want to make sure is believable, more so than any other. If this breaks down, then the rest starts to crumble. As much as I don't believe in changing goals or opportunities, I do believe you are better off reducing as needed to keep the stretch opportunity alive and reachable.

Monthly Opportunities

As you set out to make your monthly opportunities you want to align them with the objectives of your Current Year Opportunities section. A note of caution: don't try and knock it out of the park in the first month. Instead, realize that often things pick up momentum as the year progresses. Rarely, if ever, will you set out to reach an opportunity and have it equally divided into twelve chunks. However, if you write something down here you may realize that one of your Current Year Opportunities is unrealistic, so this is a great time to go back and change as needed. Keeping with the theme, some Monthly Opportunities you may have could be:

- My company will have a sales pipeline valued at over $3,000,000
- My company has monthly sales of $200,000
- I have $150,000 in cash and investments
- My wife and I have saved $7,000 this month
- We have a plan in place to have a credit score of 740 or greater
- We paid down $2,000 on our debt this month

Again, you want to be aspirational on these, but you don't want to look at these on the 15th of the month and wonder what the heck you were thinking. That'll probably happen, but you want to minimize making monthly changes. In fact, with each section you should be seeing the need to tighten up your opportunities to increase the success rate.

Weekly Opportunities

As I look at my Monthly Opportunities, I want to do a bit of a shift here from what I said with how you tackle the Monthly and Current Year Opportunities. When working on yearly attainment we have twelve months to grow into the achievement. With monthly attainment we have thirty days; a little over four weeks. That means you need to hit these opportunities hard and try to attain them quickly as each week is about 25% of your month. Get cracking on these opportunities fast so you can see where you can adjust in your long-term plan. Some of your Weekly Opportunities may look like:

- My company closed $75,000 in sales this week
- We found five new opportunities for our sales pipeline this week
- Total increase to the sales pipeline is $200,000 this week with a total of $2,600,000
- My wife and I saved $2,500 this week
- We paid down $1,000 toward our debt this week

I really want to stretch and push at this point, I want to see early success. The earlier success is seen, the more the momentum flows.

Daily Opportunities

I love my Daily Opportunities. I set these the night before, as I want time to think about these as I get ready for bed and as I sleep. I want to hit the ground running in the morning, I do not want to wake up and have to contemplate what I may or may not do. I believe by doing this, you are more likely to sleep less and wake excited to get started. After all you want to nail down these opportunities as quickly as you can! Some of the Daily Opportunities you might consider could be:

- Close out XYZ Company proposal worth $30,000
- Set up meeting with Acme to go over proposal and close for next steps
- Find two new sales opportunities valued at $100,000
- Discuss with my wife when to transfer funds to savings and what debt to pay

Like the Weekly Opportunities, I want to get on these ASAP and nail them down before the day starts to slip away.

Hourly Opportunities

If you haven't done so you should watch Ed Mylett's video on YouTube titled, "This is the GREATEST THING You Can Do Every Morning!" Although the entire video is very good, I was most interested when he spoke of breaking his days out into three six-hour days. His argument is by breaking your days down into six-hour chunks you can get more done as you shrink the finish line and sprint through the day. By condensing your normal 24-hour days down, you'll get the same amount done in a third of the time. As Ed says, he uses the first day to get everything essential out of the way. I use it to cover everything in the day that's of highest importance. That means client needs, sales prospecting or other important tasks that need to be done right away. Day 2 he uses for fun, meetings, memories, phone calls and other activities. I tend to use this for meetings, phone calls and other important tasks. Day 3 he uses for his relationships, emails, work and more meetings. I use mine for personal needs as well as providing service to others and, well, more work.

Some final thoughts on Ed's comments from the video I believe are worth mentioning, by running mini days you get a compounding effect and get more done. Secondly, after each hour quickly stop and assess how the time was used and whether you need to do a reset or adjustment. By doing this, you can get your efforts back on track quickly.

Ed asks, how different would your life be by getting three times more done than you currently do?

I opted to follow Ed's outline because it's that good and anything else I tried didn't meet the measure of what he outlined. There are a few tweaks that I've made, but for the most part I use it as he outlined—though my day normally starts at 4:00 AM, not 6:00 AM like his!

My Daily Affirmaction

This ties into the Affirmaction chapter. It's a small statement of affirmation tied together with what action I'll take to make that a reality. One recent Affirmaction I wrote was, "I have opportunities, not problems. I find solutions to my opportunities. My mood impacts my actions and outcomes. I choose to affirm my moods positively"

What I Learned Today

This provides me a moment to reflect on knowledge gained. It also serves notice that the expectation is set to learn something new every day!

Today's Success

Much like the above, this provides me a moment to reflect on the successes of the day. It's an opportunity to show gratitude for what has happened. Even on a day that's gone badly, this is the chance to see what went right, even if that is something small. I would still rather end the day thinking about the good than the bad.

Special Notes

Now, for some final thoughts. There's a highlight under each six-hour time block—this isn't part of Ed Mylett's plan, but I've added it to provide an overview of the six-hour day. I provide notes and rate the six-hour day.

At the bottom of the sheet there's the chance to rate the day, which I do in decimal points. I want to say the day was a 7.8 vs. calling it an 8 or maybe even a 7. We need to think more deeply about how we rate what we do. Lastly, you complete the sheet with why you gave it that rating.

I save my sheets and store them in the cloud so I can look over them in the future as needed. I may want to see the Affirmactions or specific improvements over time.

Final Thoughts

You will fall short using this system—it happens to me all the time, but it's nothing to worry about. I often see people create some program and then talk about it as absolute, to which I say either they're exceptional or not fully forthcoming. I tend to wear my vulnerabilities like a badge of honor. Few people push life to the limit like I do. That may sound arrogant and maybe it is, but it's how I see it. And that said, I screw things up all the time. The objective with anything like this is to improve and to reach your goals, objectives and greatest opportunities quickly. It's better for you to see the failure we are collectively than for you to feel you are failing alone. Someone sucks right along with you! Now let's just all work on sucking less.

Pills

1. Are you really ready to commit to the Opportunity Pipeline? That means tracking hourly and being vigilant with your time. It means digging in and preserving. Get your Opportunity Pipeline set up today.
2. Commit to not going to sleep at night until you have tomorrow's opportunities set up and broken out hourly.

3. Commit to running your Opportunity Pipeline up the pole daily. In the morning look at what you need to do hourly, then feel what you need to do for the day, then the week. Can you feel it happening? Do the same for the month and year. Feel yourself already completing those items. Then, dream and visualize on your "My Present State" section. Commit to doing it!

15 INTRODUCTION OPPORTUNITY BOARDS

Over the years, many of my family members would suggest we get together and create vision boards. Sitting around with magazines and printed paper discussing all the possibilities, laughing and enjoying ourselves was always fun. I would take my vision board, put it somewhere prominently in my bedroom so I could see it regularly. It would include items such as health, financial, relationship, business and items like cars, houses and boats. All things I envisioned for my life.

At first, I might have looked at it here and there, but I really didn't own what was on the board. Months went by and I didn't give it more than a passing glance. When I did look at it there were more questions than answers. What did I mean when I put that up there? Why is that up there, did I really want that? I had so little ownership of what was on the board that I deemed the whole thing meaningless. I left it up and ignored it, afraid to throw it away, feeling that doing so would cause some cosmic catastrophe in my life or create instant bad karma. Best to leave it be collecting dust.

Creation of the Opportunity Boards

While having a discussion with my wife, feeling somewhat solemn and fearful of speaking ill of the vision board I reverently whispered, "I think there might be a way to make vision boards more useful."

As discussed in the previous chapter, I had created an extremely useful tracking system called the Opportunity Pipeline. While brushing my teeth and looking at my vision board I realized that the opportunities I had developed for myself didn't match my vision board. I had inadvertently created an incongruent message. How could my vision of things come true if it didn't match my opportunities?

Once I was aware of this, I set out to design what I wanted in what I termed an Opportunity Board. There are four key areas in my life that I track within my Opportunity Pipeline: spiritual, health, financial and relationships. The latter is more specific to how my wife and I live, treat and support each other's growth. My Opportunity Board idea quickly morphed into several Opportunity Boards that broke down into those four pillars.

Each Opportunity Board covers a twelve-month period and is full of visual representations of the items in my Opportunity Pipeline. These are areas where I can take action and see progress as it's being made. Progress is tracked within the Opportunity Pipeline; the Opportunity Board provides a visual representation of my success or shortcomings.

The relationship pillar and linked Opportunity Board had to be developed specifically with my wife; that had to be our Opportunity Board. It had to be one that we both agreed upon and gravitated toward. It had to be something we could refer to that sets and directs us, it had to push us forward to our collective greater good.

Like my Opportunity Pipeline, a key area of focus within the

Opportunity Boards are the yearly opportunity focuses. The pipeline and board must match. As mentioned, throughout the day I look at the pipeline and consider the opportunities I'm working on. The view of the Opportunity Pipeline tends to gravitate to what I need to accomplish today or this week, and whether that matches up to the month. The yearly opportunity review gets a look and review on the pipeline twice a day.

Branding Your Thoughts to Your Opportunities

Likewise, the Opportunity Board is reviewed twice a day; once when I wake up and once prior to going to bed. Repetitive review of the opportunities is what makes success a likely outcome. Creating a vision board, at least for me, was more of a wishing or fantasy board. I needed a "Rubber meets the road" board.

In addition to creating the Opportunity Pipeline and Opportunity Board, it's important to brand these within your thoughts and memories. I need a reminder or a reset throughout the day where I pause and say, "What are my financial opportunities?" For example, I may say, "ABC Company has done $1,000,000 in revenue of which $150,000 was paid to me. DEF Company has done $2,000,000 in revenue of which $250,000 was paid to me. My family is debt free. Our investments have increased by X percent this year." Having this branded onto my thoughts and mind allows me to access it and use it as needed. Imagine a bad day—you've just found out you lost a project you were sure was coming to your company. At that moment you feel down, perhaps even defeated. Having that sort of information branded on your thoughts allows you to access it when you need it. It allows you to take positive information, treat it as already received, and give thanks for it. You are doing a real time reset on your most important opportunities.

Imagine doing that for your relationships. My wife and I have discussions how our frequency radiates to and through each other because we're working on the same opportunities. We discuss the dates we've had, the vacations taken, and the laughs and memories made. All spoken as if we've already done it. A fantastic outcome of this is the increase in flowers I buy my wife and the uptick in verbal and physical affection we show.

Giving Gratitude for What We Will Receive

Each morning and evening I give my prayers in thanks for receiving those things into my life, for God's help in guiding me as I attained them, and ask how I can continue to best use what I have for others. It may seem strange to pray as if I have already received, but when we're told there is no beginning and there no end it makes perfect sense that I can pray as if something has already been received.

As I go to sleep at night, I provide to my subconscious a task to work on while I sleep, since the subconscious mind never rests. I only provide it one item to solve; over time I will define it consciously for my needs. I always go over every pillar in my head, speaking as if I have received it. I give gratitude for the acceptance of it. Finally, once ready to fall asleep I focus on the one task I've given my subconscious to solve and I concentrate on that until I fall asleep. I constantly see what I can get my mind to do and how far I can push it.

One area of focus for me is increasing revenue for my company. I told my subconscious mind that we needed to increase revenue and thus increase the amount of opportunities we have in the sales pipeline. The focused task I gave the subconscious was to find the company revenue. From this, I had a dream where a peer introduced me to a man looking to fund us. He decided against doing so but was so impressed with what we had accomplished that he wrote us a check for $2,300,000! I woke up happy, as you can imagine because that's a pretty awesome dream. Mostly, I realized that although that wasn't increasing revenue, my subconscious was making a concerted effort to solve the problem. I took a moment and gave thanks for the dream and the efforts made on my behalf by my subconscious mind.

The more we're able to imprint our greatest opportunities onto our minds, the more likely it is that we'll succeed at achieving them. We become more aware of what we need to do daily. We start to see opportunities placed in our path that will help us reach our desired outcomes. These are opportunities that have always been there, but they go unnoticed because we're not focused on them.

My challenge to you is to start with one Opportunity Board from the four pillars, and then build it based on your yearly objectives. If you are mid-year, feel free to make an eighteen-month Opportunity Board. The idea is to present something measurable and attainable to yourself, something you can build action around. Match it to your Opportunity Pipeline. Put it to memory and start living what your greatest opportunities are. Feel free to focus on one, or to do as many as you feel you can handle. The idea is to build momentum and to use this as a repetitive reminder to help you reach your opportunities.

Pills

1. Your first action is to align your Opportunity Boards with your Opportunity Pipeline. Make sure the you have a clear vision of the Opportunity Board.
2. Take the Opportunity Pipeline and create an Opportunity Board for each area mentioned. Remember, this is for the year.
3. Each morning as you wake, and each evening before you sleep study and feel each Opportunity Board. Visualize what you have to do tomorrow to meet your Opportunity Pipeline and how it impacts the boards.

16 MARKETING AND SELLING OURSELVES

A colleague of mine, someone who has been a client, peer and subcontractor to our company over the years had an emotional crisis. He's been through a lot; he's in a position where things are just beating him down. He recently lost a family member, suffered through a divorce and has had difficulties finding new employment. He's living with friends as he gets back on his feet and he's questioning almost everything.

He assisted us with a project and commented to me that he felt he wasn't doing his best work. Before speaking with him I asked the project manager how he was doing, and the response was that the client loved him and his work, they were very impressed with what he found, and that he communicated better with the project manager than most of our employees and subcontractors.

As the two of us spoke I asked him, "Where do you feel you are lacking in quality of work?"

He responded, "I don't have one thing to point at and there hasn't been anything the client said, in fact they say they're happy. But I can't help thinking they're either not forthcoming or that I'm missing something."

Selling Yourself Even When You Feel Unworthy

There was something he was missing, and it became crystal clear to me.

I asked him if I could tell him about the past several years at my company. As I told him about the massive debt, the fear and doubt, the thought that I was useless and a fraud, he was shocked. He wanted to know how I kept it together, and how he never knew about it. My response was that nobody cared, people didn't want me to suffer, but they didn't want to hear about it. I had kept myself going and convinced everyone around me that I was doing just fine.

What he was missing was the need to market himself.

When we're beaten, we tend to wear that all over our countenance. It's like the black plague; we think it's hidden but it exudes from us and is visible to others. We may be able to hide it for a bit, but if people spend enough time with us it'll show up. It did so for him repeatedly during job interviews, and I had seen it in action. Since he didn't even know it was there, he wasn't working to manage it or remove it all together.

I asked him what he thought interviews saw when they looked at him. He talked about his pedigree, education, certifications, industry knowledge and strong references.

I asked again, and he admitted that he didn't understand. So, I told him what I saw: a man beaten, head down and tilted, shoulders tucked in and breathing shallowly. He sounded like someone who knew what he was saying but wasn't buying it himself. There was no confidence in himself and therefore, they had no confidence in him. If he was lucky, he could get past the recruiter in the first interview. If he was really lucky, he would get past the second person. However, given that he was seeking an executive position, eventually the ruse would be up and they would realize that he just didn't measure up to their requirements for a person leading an extremely important group.

He responded that he didn't want to be misleading and present himself as something he wasn't. There it was—a belief that he was that person. Beaten, down and out, and of little value. My question to him was this: if you get the job you interview for, how would that impact and change your life? Paint me a picture of the person you would be and the things you could do. He smiled, a bit of joy thinking about it as he outlined what he would do to integrate his proven practices, his team development, his reporting and vision delivery to executive leadership and on and on. Personally, he could rebuild his life, get his own place and start to be social again.

My next question stopped him. Which person are they getting when you start the job, the guy that's beaten and down or the guy that just outlined everything with confidence?

That's when it clicked. My hope is that he remembers this and can project himself as he is, not as he's been beaten up to believe.

The Real Man I Am

No one wanted to see the beaten man I was during my struggles, other than maybe the attorney and psychologist I was seeing. My wife loved me, my children loved me, my friends at least pretended to like me and on occasion I even loved and liked myself. But none of them wanted to see me as a beaten man. None of them wanted to hear me whine about how bad things were. I knew it firsthand; I hated hearing myself and would get frustrated by my lack of ability to manage my emotions. Let's be clear, when I'm at my best, I love the sound of my voice. I believe others like me that way too. Equally, when I'm off I don't want to hear what I have to say, so the assumption is fair that no one else really wants to hear that. Who would?

Even during all of that, the whining and worrying wasn't the real me. That wasn't the guy I knew, and it wasn't the guy everyone else knew. The person I wasn't needed to be was shelved for the person I had to be— the guy that constantly worried and secretly whined had to stay hidden during working hours. When you are rebuilding a company, most waking hours are working hours. That meant my friend couldn't see the fake and fearful me; he had to see the real me that was being forced out and paraded front and center for everyone else.

He was the guy that was going to turn this company around, he was the one capable of rebuilding and growing the company. He was the one people knew and loved. Sometimes it felt a little like that movie Weekend at Bernie's, but with imaginary friends holding me up so I could make it through the day. It meant constant pep talks to myself. It meant prepping for that meeting by making sure I was strong, in control and capable. Then, and only as needed, I would let the whining and worrying guy out for a bit. But only for a bit, then he was shelved again.

Presenting Yourself When You Don't Feel Presentable

We all have times when we feel less than our best. When we're going through something significant, that tends to last for extended periods and we can start to feel like it's the new normal.

My head would spin and I would look at my situation in its entirety, with every potential outcome playing out negatively. It was always one negative thought leading to the next, spiderwebbing out to an unending number of negative outcomes. That's how it felt, like my entire world was crashing down around me. This sounds melodramatic, and maybe it was. At times it was all I could do to drag my sorry carcass out of bed and into clothing so I could leave for the day. But, that's exactly what I needed to do—and it's what you need to do as well.

The tough love I would tell myself is that there are people out there with serious issues, much more serious than what we have going on. People whose normal is our abnormal. People in countries that don't have the basic things we expect to sustain life. I mean, through it all I was never homeless, and always had my mobile phone, a laptop, family, food, a bed and many other things many people just don't have. Yes, I had people coming down on me with demands and threats and that's not easy to handle, but I could have walked away from it all and started over. I created my pain; I chose my pain and I was going to get myself out of my pain. I owned the pain.

Every day, we each need to get it together and set the stage for what we're about to do throughout the day. As I navigated through this mess, I found that I had to remind myself every morning to get motivated and prepared to deliver. I told myself that I was still standing, that I rose yesterday and delivered, that today I rose and would deliver and tomorrow and the following day I would rise and deliver. I also told myself that today I'm stronger than yesterday, and tomorrow I'm stronger than today. There were times I drove down the freeway screaming at myself to wake up and tell myself I could accomplish anything that anyone put in front of me. I yelled that I had handled everything that had been put in front of me so far, and that I would handle anything coming my way.

That sounds like a totally ego driven, testosterone filled rant of a man with low self-esteem. Well, pretty much. That was my point in doing it. I didn't have the unwavering belief in myself that I have now. I was beaten, I was in recovery and I was doing what I needed. That meant looking like a lunatic yelling and driving down the freeway. I would walk in the office and yell, "Yeah! Let's do this! Anyone want a piece of this because I'm on fire!" If I wanted others to believe it, I had to believe it. After a drive like that how could I not?

Living with the Subconscious Mind

In his book 'The Master Key System', Charles Haanel talks about how our subconscious mind is in control of our mind 90% of the time. I immediately questioned this—but if a person slept eight hours a day and commuted two, that covers roughly 42% of the day. Throw in time cooking, eating, bathing, watching TV and many other activities where we're not consciously thinking, and it doesn't take long to see that 90% might not be too much of a stretch. Even as I type this, I don't consciously think where the letters are on the keyboard, but my hand is typing away with subconscious fury.

It's been mentioned several times in this book, but it needs repeating until this sinks into your subconscious. What your conscious mind tells your subconscious mind matters. For ten percent of your life, through the conscious mind, you are impacting seemingly mindless time with either good or bad information. Most of us tend to run negative and worry, which means we're sending the message to our subconscious mind that it needs to focus on the negative and worry as it attempts to solve problems that are most often imaginary. It is imperative to your mental wellbeing and your success that your subconscious mind hears only positive information or at the least a tilt more positive than negative.

In an effort to market yourself to others, you must first market you to yourself. You must learn to believe that you are true greatness. That may seem farfetched, but it's not. You are truly great. We all are. Training our conscious to feed our subconscious mind takes practice and training. It takes us having negative thoughts, realizing it, and changing them to positive ones. It means, when you are doubting yourself, stop and tell yourself of your true greatness.

This may sound like a cheerleader, and perhaps that's the case, but cheer yourself on and prepare yourself to deliver on your greatness.

Pills

1. Ask family and friends to give an unbiased and direct assessment of how you market yourself to them and others.
2. Can you see where you need to make improvements?
3. What can you do to prepare yourself before meeting with someone, so they see the best of you?
4. How can you better market yourself to most important person there is—you?

17 BUILDING AND KEEPING THE MOMENTUM

At the time of writing this, it's nearly 4:00 PM on the Friday between Christmas and the New Year. This is a time where things slow down, and we reflect and show our gratitude. We feel the peace and joy of the season, we sit back and soak it all in and use the time to recharge our batteries. It seems like the entire world has stopped. I'm not sure where it went, but it doesn't seem like anyone else is working. I even had one client ask that we hold off on submitting any more information until the 2nd of January. They just wanted to relax and not think about work. That's fine but come the 2nd it's all getting dumped on your lap.

Momentum Swings Hot and Cold

Regardless of where you are right now—fixing your life, fixing your business, fully engaged in life or in your business or taking it easy and coasting—you should be hyperaware of the momentum you are gaining or losing. Nothing sits still. The idea of letting something sit for a while and coming back to it assumes things will stay the same.

They don't.

As a small company, each person wears multiple hats. It's not unusual for me to focus on recruiting, project management, client satisfaction, employee satisfaction, government regulation and selling. Driving revenue for the company is the lifeblood of any organization. Other things are important, but without a constant flow of revenue and business, you have no business. Prior to the unraveling of my company I thought I could take my eye off selling—after all I had two fully dedicated salespeople doing the selling for me.

Nothing could have been more untrue.

Momentum needed to shift from doing, to managing and training. Taking my eye off selling meant the need to shift the direction of the momentum didn't occur.

Where Do You Need a Constant Flow of Momentum?

There are five key areas of your life: relationships, finances, health, spiritual and entertainment. You need to determine where you spend your time and what deserves the push for momentum. In Stephen Covey's book, "The 7 Habits of Highly Effective People," he talks about juggling balls and that some can drop and they bounce, while others are made of glass and when they fall they break. You need to determine which of the five areas if dropped, will break and not bounce.

Forget any grand ideas of balance. It isn't always realistic or sustainable. I spend very little time on entertainment; do I really want to balance that in my life? Of those four things left for me, relationships, finances, health and spiritual each gets a portion of my time and that varies depending on what's important in the moment and at each stage of my life. My children are all adults, they don't need or want me around as much as they did, and frankly I don't have the energy or desire to watch them play a sport or other activity anymore. Not to mention, it would be weird! The momentum and focus I have today needs to be mostly directed at my wife, and to a lesser degree my children and grandchildren. My momentum is focused on making my wife's life as amazing and fulfilling as I possibly can.

Health is one of those areas for me that I let drop, thinking I would focus on it later. Thankfully, the ball bounced. Now I'm doing all I can to right many of the wrongs I inflicted on my body for years. Momentum is something I experienced with my health in a big way. Momentum doesn't necessarily mean it's good, just that you are moving in a direction—any direction. Momentum shifting in a positive direction takes force, thought, and a lot of action. It also takes a lot of patience. Needing to lose 100 pounds doesn't happen overnight, but you still want to see results quickly anyway. It's pretty much like anything in life, but this part has a scale.

Most likely you'll require a constant shift between needs that demand your attention. You can try to balance momentum, but that's impossible. When you focus on one area the others start to slip backwards, and that's why Covey's analogy of juggling balls is a great visual. You grab one, while throwing another into the air while the third is on its way down. None of those balls are in motion in the same direction. As I take time to focus on writing, areas within spiritual, relationships and health are all taking a backseat and thus the momentum stops or slows.

There is truth that momentum can continue to flow when you take time to focus on other areas and I want to mention this briefly. There are things you can do that keep things moving forward, sometimes for a long time with little effort if you've already built enough momentum. If you've made a lot of money and have invested well, those investments can carry on the momentum for you. Likewise, if you choose to exercise and eat a proper diet your body can continue its momentum while in recovery. If you have meaningful discussions, be they with a true friend or your partner, your relationships can continue forward with momentum. However, if left alone for too long, everything slips back.

When managing the recovery of my company it required high levels of action and momentum, to the point where other things had to take a backseat. Over time as the momentum started carrying itself and needed more guidance and less force, I was able to turn my focus more fully back to other areas. It's important that you build those areas up now so when you do need to focus elsewhere you won't find an empty cup. Spiritually, I pulled from that cup often and drained it down—not completely, but it did suffer.

So, remember, when you focus high levels of energy and drive momentum forward in one area, other areas take a hit.

Seeking a Series of Success

If you find yourself in need of momentum, there are several places where you can start. You'll require levels of patience and triumph, enjoying those small wins, until you've delivered enough force to sustain momentum. It'll take a series of successes for you to recognize and gain your ground in any endeavor. Here are some areas that will help.

Be careful where you get your advice. I see people that will put critical needs out to the masses on social media asking for help. In response I see people that have no business giving advice providing it, and doing so poorly. Not just one person, but many, giving knee jerk responses to things the know little to nothing about. Seek advice from two or three people that have expertise in each area. As an example, if you need marital advice, you are better off getting it from people that have been married awhile and are happy. Why go to someone unhappily married, regardless of time, for advice? You also want to make sure your advice comes from people that have accomplished more than you, regardless of age or years of experience. The same is true in business, health and finances, seek out great advice.

Focus on where your greatest needs are. During my business issues I focused on what mattered most. That meant someone else could mow the lawn and maintain the cars at home. At work, that meant someone else could do those other items that took me away from driving revenue into the company. I was selling, not mowing the lawn or other tasks I could farm out. It's all about production and producing the right things at the right level. Momentum was needed and revenue created more of it than anything. You need to guard your time and make sure you are not using it on busy activities instead of critical ones.

Add more OPT, Other Peoples Time, as quickly as possible. If, like me, your most important need is driving revenue, find ways to use OPT. You can do that through partnerships, hiring salespeople or automate by using tools like Google Ads—and yes, I know automation isn't OPT unless we consider artificial intelligence to be people! At our company I started looking around the office at who might have a little time to help drive revenue. One of our largest projects last year came from someone with no experience, but a willingness to jump in. Momentum requires creativity.

Schedule, monitor, track and guard your calendar. I mention this in-depth in the Opportunity Pipeline chapter of this book, and I'll say it in a few words here. Be obsessed about guarding your time, achieving small wins and staying on task. Do not waste your time. Don't waste it playing games and don't waste it doing tasks that don't need to be done. If you schedule your time tightly, stay committed to it and monitor your success. Be mindful of time thieves. They show up anywhere from the person needing you to do something that only takes 2 minutes (it always takes more) to the office co-worker that suggests mid-afternoon lunch breaks at the billiard hall across the street. I even schedule my downtime; that way I know it's play, relax and regenerate time.

Momentum requires your view of the present, not the future.
Vision is great but looking to the future doesn't create the
momentum you need now. Unless you can tie your vision to your
current needs and momentum, don't. Focusing on the future can
overwhelm your current needs. We focused on driving revenue to
cover our monthly needs of payroll and debt reduction. If we would
have focused on the overarching debt and long-term financial needs
of the company, that could have deflated our efforts and scared us
along the way. Staying focused on the immediate needs allowed us to
have immediate momentum and results.

**Remember, your growth and momentum happen in small
spurts.** Don't be in such a hurry that you can't look up to see
progress. Some days you'll take a step backwards, but that doesn't
mean the entire momentum stalls. It means that over time, you are
growing to reach your objectives. Don't get overly caught up in the
moment. Celebrate wins and failures appropriately, don't ride one too
high or the other too low. Just recognize them and move on.

Take time for you. Each day make sure you give back to yourself.
This was one of the most difficult areas to learn, I was so focused on
the need and momentum that I neglected other areas completely.
Take time to rejuvenate, meditate, learn and exercise. The only
caution is to do them and get back to work, your momentum needs
you!

Pills

1. What activities are you involved with that are your greatest
   needs? How can you put forth the energy needed to get and
   sustain that momentum?
2. Knowing that momentum can slow when other things come
   up that need your attention, what can you do to keep the
   momentum moving and not let your foot off the gas?

3. What OPT can you use to increase your momentum and increase your focus?
4. What small bursts of momentum can you look back on and see spurred growth? Can you take a look back daily on the small bursts you achieved?

18 DARING TO DOUBLE DOWN

In blackjack, there's a term called doubling down. It's an exhilarating move that allows the gambler to take their current bet and double it in the middle of a hand, and in exchange they receive an extra card. It's normally extremely risky and usually stops your betting. The risks tend to stop more conservative gamblers from making a double down bet, while aggressive gamblers tend to double down much too often.

In business we play the double down bet as well, and much like blackjack some are timid and others adventurous. Though we need to have a strategy that allows us to maximize our efforts while minimizing our risks, there are risks to doubling down and going all in.

Doubling Down on My Company

I sat down with what was left of my management team once the dust settled with a clear objective. We had a theme for the coming years: drive revenue and pay down debt. In order to reach that goal, we had to double down in a specific area and focus. For us, that meant putting other areas on hold—for example, service and product development. We asked ourselves where the greatest value and use of time was—on the phones, or at a conference?"

This became our strategic bet. Until the debt was paid off and we were able to get back on solid footing, we needed revenue to either pay down the debt or to be reinvested into driving more revenue so we could pay down more debt. It was a vicious cycle.

The double down for us was going all in on the here and now and increasing revenue month after month so we could get on solid ground. Creating and cementing our future growth took a backseat to creating and cementing our current existence.

Although I don't frequent casinos, I am a gambler when it comes to business. That desire to gamble in business is what got us into trouble, as we had a belief that business was coming, and we would have revenue to cover the debt. It was a foolish bet—it was like asking for a hit when I was holding a king and a seven card. Not impossible, but not a good bet. Moving forward meant the risk had to be relative to the need, and the reward had to be relative to the risk. Doubling down on driving revenue and reducing the debt was a bet that seemed logical. The was in our ability to win enough hands and drive enough revenue to make more than the dealer—our current debt—did.

When Choosing to Double Down

The message of this book is about recovery, be that business or personal. With that in mind, the doubling down discussion here is about choosing to do it to get back on your feet. Once you've done this, you can look at doubling down by prioritizing long-term goals over short-term ones. But right now, it's important to prioritize the short-term over the long. Ideally, you limit the need to do this, and only do so to reach recovery.

Regardless of your need to double down you need to focus on a strategy and live it. Continuing with the real-life example of my company, that strategy was more than just driving more revenue. It had to be the right revenue for our immediate needs. That meant finding projects that we could close and access the needed funds quickly. A client had a three-week project they need to start in a week? That met our strategy. A three-week project that didn't need starting for six-months? We put that in the pipeline and monitored it. An ongoing six-month project where they paid us monthly Net 30, that required a new hire that had to be paid for 60 days before the company was? That was a hard pass. In those situations we had to be creative, but ultimately if it didn't meet the strategy then we had to pass. Doubling down means you must stick to your strategy to reduce your risk of going bust. It also removes emotions that can cloud your judgement.

How much are you willing to bet? Doubling down means you are making a hard bet on what you need to do, business or personal. Knowing just how much you are willing to bet ahead of time allows you to butt up against that bet without flinching. It also gives you a line you are not willing to cross. For us, that bet was big, and I was willing to lose even more than I had. However, as I've said, I still needed to be strategic. That bet included me not getting paid for months if needed. It meant me driving for Uber to keep the bet rolling. It meant deferring on some loans to pay others. It meant losing sleep to stay up selling. It meant knowing when to end the bet, leave my business, and go do something new. That part was hard to stomach but knowing that there was a limit kept me hungry and pushing forward.

When choosing your bet and determining the risks, make sure you are not putting all your money and effort on hope. The more options you create, the less impact one specific bet matters. Placing all your time and energy on one thing is excessively risky, so you had better make sure that's 100% sure to work. The more ongoing projects or opportunities you have, the less likely you are to feel the impact when one doesn't go your way.

When to Admit Defeat

There were times when things got extremely tight and sketchy, and we weren't sure if we would have the funds to make payroll or debt repayments. There were a few occasions when we knew funds wouldn't arrive in time to meet both, so we had to confront creditors and ask for more time. As hard as that could be, there was always a more difficult discussion we had to have with ourselves. I had told my leadership team that if the company was facing imminent death, then it needed to be addressed with me quickly. I often said to them, "We're short on cash for the next week, and it appears to me that revenue is coming to maintain our plan. It also appears to me that sales trajectory is such to continue that trend. But, am I pulling the wool over my own eyes?" The question was meant to illicit a frank discussion on the status of the plan and subsequently the company. Thankfully, as tight and as white knuckle as things had gotten, we were never in any real danger.

No one likes to admit it's time to throw in the towel. No one likes the feeling or thought of failure. But not addressing real problems doesn't derail the inevitable. Hunkering down, holding tighter to that double down and making a run at a strategy gone bad is common. Part of the plan you prepare needs to address the "What if" scenario. What if you get to this point and the plan isn't working?

A peer in a similar situation started to see his strategy of increasing revenue from a successful business unit falter when he set out to transfer and revive a failing business unit. When sales slowed, he addressed it by adding salespeople. This was contradictory to what his leadership team saw as the real need. However, there was no "What if" scenario built into their double down plan. His team stayed quiet, he added salespeople and the double down failed. In an effort to save one failing business unit he nearly lost two.

In the management world, this is known as an escalation of commitment. It's when, during a negative trajectory from poor actions or decisions, a group or individual stays the course or doubles down even more instead of changing course. People begin to act irrationally and push to justify their decision and continued action down a failed path.

I won't dive deep into protecting yourself from this, but I'll end with this: set the "What if" scenario in place ahead of time. Additionally, have rules in place that outline how governing leadership can vote on whether it's time to admit defeat or soldier on with the plan. When this time comes it's emotional, and these rules and planning will force decisions to be logical.

Pills

1. Where can you double down, take a calculated risk, and make an aggressive push toward the attainment of something that brings you value?
2. Consider this, how much are you willing to bet on your double down to risk achieving something valuable?
3. What unemotional questions can you ask of yourself that will help you make a good choice in doubling down?
4. Do you have a "What if" scenario should your double down not work? What is it? What will you do, and how will it affect your business and personal life?
5. Knowing your "What if," is it worth it? Are you willing to risk it?

19 DON'T GO IT ALONE

There's a temptation to do things yourself when faced with a crisis. You think that no one knows the trouble you are in or how to solve it better than you. Perhaps you are embarrassed because of the massive screw up you've done. Maybe you are exhausted because going through something traumatic is exhausting. Maybe you'd just like to ignore it and treat it like a hairball in the corner of the room, hoping it will go away. I went through this early on, and at many other times while recovering from my business follies. There is a temptation to shut people out.

Build a Team of Support

Whatever you are going through, you can't do everything on your own. Creating a team is paramount because you only have so much time, energy and knowledge. There simply is only so much you can do. Even if you are a powerhouse and get more done than anyone you know, you still need more people around you for support. But it's important that you build a support group of the right people. Too often people in crisis seek out others that validate their misery, when that's the last thing they need. You need people that will guide you, but always help you with logic and wisdom. You also need access to various people with different skills and understanding; don't think that one specific person is akin to a Swiss Army Knife. Your mother may love you, but most likely she can't guide you through resurrecting your company.

Here are some of the groups you need to build and nurture.

Family

Let's take a moment and appreciate our families. They love us, hate us, care for us, kick us, humor us and drive us nuts. They're a mixed bag, and since they are blood, you are mostly stuck with them. More so than any group discussed here you need to guard yourself against them. Think about your family, take a moment and go through all those that you can think of. How many of them can you say fall into middle ground? They're neither supportive, loving and caring, nor are they antagonistic, frustrating and uncaring? They're just in the middle ground, lacking an opinion or unemotional when it comes to you. Have any of those? Me neither.

You need your family for moral support. Take the best of them and use them to buoy you up emotionally. Cry on their shoulder. Let them hold you and tell you everything will be alright. Who knows, they may even be right! Use them when you need to let it all out and have a pity party. They're the ones that you can allow to see you at your worst.

And as for your more negative family members? Compartmentalize them. Be nice to them at social gatherings, but unless they're going to carry you and build you up don't bother with any more than that. This may seem harsh, but we're talking about getting you back to where you need to be.

Remember, they're good at certain things, they can help you in certain ways, but they can't help you in every way.

Friends

It's during these times of crisis that you look around and ask where all your friends went. Most likely, you'll have a select few—I had two. Unlike my family, they wouldn't allow me to have a pity party, and nor did I want one I would let my guard down a bit, show my emotions, but always with a plan of how I would address problems.

True friends should be there to guide you to where you need to be, with as much force as they know you can handle in the moment. I remember speaking with one friend about our businesses tax issue early on and how much it was eating at me. His comment was, "The IRS will get every cent you owe them, don't think for a minute they won't. They're also not going to do anything crazy to stand in the way of you paying that back. You have more leverage than you realize, without you focused they won't get their money as quickly." His goal was probably twofold: get me to shut up and stop whining and more importantly, get my head in the game. True friends won't coddle you. They'll let you bend a bit, show some emotions, tell your story and then they're going to want to get you back on your feet.

You can have a friendship where you go to a game, get your mind off things. Maybe shopping if you are into that. You can't have friends that want you to go out partying, drinking or general debauchery. Those aren't friends, they're party people. You also want to stay clear of negative people; you don't need those friends right now. In fact, you never need them. This is about getting you on top of your mountain, not down in some ditch.

Business

If you are a solopreneur going it alone seems to be your only choice. If you have employees you should know how crucial it is to have a tight plan organized, and why you need to get others to assist you. As either a solopreneur or someone with employees, you'll need to leverage others in business in order to get back on your feet.

These people are not your friends, and they're not your family. If they are friends and family, you need to segment that part of your life off from your business life. They need to see a powerhouse. My recommendation is that you treat them as business associates, and not your confidants. These people may count on you for their livelihood, and you want them to see you have your game together. They need to see strength, fortitude and direction. They don't need to see you running around and screaming that the sky is falling. They need you to keep it together and have a plan.

Now, as for you solopreneurs, you'll need to let your fingers off of a few things; loosen that grip and give some things up. This is about getting back on your feet, this isn't about control. Consider where you can subcontract out what doesn't drive revenue to others. Think of bookkeeping, janitorial or housekeeping, mowing your own lawn—whatever you can offload so you can focus on what you do well.

Clear and Defined Company Goals

Undoubtedly your best employees are aware that the company, and potentially you personally, need fixing. Make sure you have clearly defined company goals to give the team direction on how they can help you and the company. No goals means no good direction, and mayhem may ensue. You'll want to direct them with short and long-term targets, where they can have real results that are measurable.

Clearly Communicate Your Vision and Plan

This aligns with the defined company goals. Often goals are set and people head off to accomplish with no reporting structure is in place. Reporting goes up and down the leadership ladder, as you need employees to communicate clearly their needs and how they are progressing. Likewise, they need to hear from you how others and the company in general are doing. As the leader, you need to know when to be a cheerleader and pump the company up, and when to relay the gravity of the situation.

Let Others Set Their Own Goals as They Pertain to the Vision and Plan

You want others to feel invested in the vision and plan, so let them create and guide their direction within that plan. Not only does it give them ownership of what they're doing, but it may bridge a gap you've created from the business pitfalls. Letting them have the space to create and deliver will build confidence in both themselves and in you. It'll also free you up for the next part.

Focus on What You do Well

You need to pinpoint your efforts if you are to reach these goals. For me, that's selling and driving revenue. For example, I tried doing project management, but I struggled. It left me spread too thin and I hated it. As a friend of mine constantly reminds me, "Stay in your lane." You need to do this so you can reach your goals quickly and get back up and running.

Again, these aren't the people you show your weakness and emotions to. They're the people that need to see the powerhouse.

Peer Group

A peer group is a group of individuals that share common objectives and similarities. In a business peer group, they are often business owners and leaders that have a revenue range, employees and often come from varying types of business that don't directly compete. They meet regularly, maybe once a month, and share ideas, problems and successes.

An advantage to a peer group is that the likelihood of someone in the group having experienced something like you is high. Very few, if any, will have reached where they are without pitfalls and roadblocks. This means you will have people with experience that can guide you and provide direction. They'll also be able to empathize and can provide you a proper level of emotional support. You'll find motivation here that will often give you the peace of mind and energy to tackle your problems.

Peer groups also allow you the opportunity to help others with their problems, which will provide you with insight into your own. Serving others, even if it is just through listening and offering advice, often provides us with a respite from our own troubling thoughts. As your peers open up about what they're experiencing, you'll quickly learn that you are in a safe place. What is talked about in a peer group is confidential and never leaves the group.

Finally, what you need to take away from your peer group experience is that when your peers guide you, they expect you to be accountable to them. You must report back and let them know that their time spent helping you meant something and was appreciated.

Other Support Avenues

This list isn't all encompassing, but what's outlined will combine to cover your primary needs. But there are also church groups, meetups, physiologists and others that can help.

Patient, Pliable and Grateful

Making the decision to go all in and allow others to help you means you will have a learning curve and they may too. Handing over the reins regarding details will require you to let go of control in order to take control of the bigger picture. You need to be patient with people that are helping, as they may not help exactly the way you need it or as quickly as you would like. You'll also need patience with yourself as you get used to this new way of including others. You will need to be pliable to situations and needs and adapting as needed to reach your objectives. It is about the end result and the journey getting there. Both are important!

Look After Others That Look After You

Something dawned onto me one day, almost every discussion I was having with people had to do with my needs. Either they were helping me emotionally or with my business needs, but most of the discussions nearly always revolved around me. This is understandable; if you have an open wound then you need a little more care. But others have needs too, so make sure you take time to look after them. Make time to only speak about them and really listen. I found that people were much more likely to help me if they knew that each time I spoke to them, it wasn't just about me and my problems.

Final Thoughts

Enlisting the help of others and leaning on them doesn't mean you are weak. It means you are smart because you are willing and able to pull together a team to help you. It means you are strong because you can push aside your pride and show humility. It means you are formidable because people are willing to get behind you as you lead the charge. It means you are likable and believable because people are joining you. Remember this: the weak fold up, go home and move on. The strong roll up their sleeves, push through the pain and solve problems. If you are reading this, you are strong.

Pills

1. Take time and assess your family and friends. Which can you lean on appropriately for the highest and most appropriate level of support?

2. In business, where and who can you lean on? Who can help you?
3. Where else can you get support? Church, peer groups, etc.?
4. Build a list of your support team so you know exactly who to turn to when you need specific assistance.
5. Who can you help? Who can you be a good team member to?

20 CONFRONTING YOUR DOUBT AND FACING YOUR FEARS

One constant in trying to turn my company around was fear, especially early on. Fear of the hard money lender, IRS, the other people we owed money to, making payroll, paying our outstanding monthly requirements, driving revenue, and pretty much anything and everything else that came to mind. Fear gripped me; it was my constant companion. In a fraction of a second, I could go from completely calm to a raving lunatic, panicking about whatever thought was darting through my mind. I was a mess of fear-based living.

Living in Faith

Today, one constant is in my life is living in faith. I have faith that we can make payroll, I'll get paid regularly, the monthly requirements needed to run the business will be made, that revenue goals will be attained and all will be fine. Now, rather than fear, faith grips me; it's my constant companion. When a negative thought comes into my head, I can stop myself before it has a chance to grow and change fear to faith quickly. When a thought darts through my head it's pleasant. I'm now living a faith-based life.

As with everything in life, we come to a crossroad. In one direction there is the path of fear, in the other the path of faith. For every decision, great or small, we make this choice consciously or unconsciously. When we wake in the morning, we unconsciously make the decision to get out of bed and get ready for the day, and we live with the faith that we are able to do this without failure crossing our path. There is no "what if". When we get in the car to drive the conscious and unconscious cross—we consciously look for foot traffic and cars as we back into the street, but we unconsciously make our daily commute with little thought. Here, there is slightly more awareness of the choice we have between faith and fear. Faith gets us there safely; awareness helps us stop at red lights to keep the fear impulse at bay.

As I wrote this, I received a message from a candidate that said, "Tab, I'm extremely disappointed to say the least. I understand it's a mistake, but I'll be contacting the company directly about the salary now." I have two paths—the path of fear and the path of faith. I could sit here and think that the client is going to be really upset and might not do business with us moving forward. I should have checked the numbers more closely. Alternatively, I could tell myself that mistakes happen and worrying about how the client might or might not react doesn't help me.

It's these moments where we have to make a decision: am I going to choose faith or fear? When we choose fear, we choose the path of overreacting and creating outcomes that aren't real. In fact, had I chosen any of those fear-based responses I would have been wrong. I received an email from the client that read: "I got finance to approve the higher amount, the candidate has verbally accepted. Let's chalk this one up to missing documentation…we're very happy with the work and volume you produce and look forward to working with you in the future." What a waste that would have been to choose fear over faith.

Fear is a Choice

Do I mean you must literally ask yourself, "Am I going to choose faith or fear?" Yes, if that's the basis for getting past the knee jerk reaction to turn to fear. Fear is a choice; it exists only as we view things in the future. It's nothing more than a perception, one that likely doesn't exist. We're not talking about literal fear, like if we were being chased by a bear. We are talking about the irrational fear your mind creates over what ifs and possibilities. But really, what's the worst that could happen? I've managed to eclipse 20,000 days on this earth, and I've overcome every fear that's crossed my path. Some I've overcome while figuratively crapping my pants, others I've overcome wielding a sword of strength. That's why, on occasion, I still ask myself, "Am I going to choose faith or fear?" When I choose faith, I choose to wield a sword. When I choose to fear I choose to crap myself. How's that for a mental picture to move you to faith!

The Magic 8 Ball of Faith

If you are familiar with a Magic 8 Ball toy, each comes with a die that has 20 faces with answers that are affirmative, negative and non-committal. You ask a yes or no question and the response comes back with one of 20 responses—and you can just keep asking until you get the response you want! With fear we're just using the Magic 8 Ball with only five of the responses. You ask the same question and you receive "Don't count on it, My reply is no, My sources say no, Outlook not so good or Very doubtful." With fear we keep shaking, asking the same question and getting one of the five responses, only to shake harder and quicker. We start to ask other questions that stem off the first, and still we receive the same five responses. So, we shake harder and quicker, firing off more questions as our fear increases.

I bet you didn't know this. The Magic 8 ball has five negative replies and ten affirmative ones. Often, we're so fixated on the negative that we don't see the joy that surround us. With the Magic 8 Ball of faith you can ask any question and you'll receive an answer that sounds very much like "All signs point to yes." That's faith we can start to build on!

Choosing to Live a Fear Based Life

I'm in a group of professionals and one individual sent me a message that read, "How do you rebound from setbacks? I recently had a heartbreaking loss and I'm gripped by fear and have little motivation. I can't stop dwelling on the past."

My response was this.

Sorry for the setback, those things suck. I have definitely had my share in life. I find the only way I can get over them is by jumping into something and getting back at it. I need to build, be productive and see advances. Not that I can expect 100% at the start, but I have to start where I am. At the end of the day I need to look back and see I worked hard, pushed forward, walked through quicksand (that's what it feels like) and had one productive day. That's all I'm after, one productive day. Then, the next day I'm looking to repeat and have one good day. I did this for about three years once. The positive is that I can handle pretty much any setback that comes my way because of those trials. So, there is one huge win for you if you come out the other side handling this instead of it handling you. As you go through this, you have to consciously push fear out of your thoughts. Fear will grip you quickly and choke you quicker, with fear you cannot accomplish what I've outlined in the time you need to get things done."

He said to me that getting rid of fear felt like a dream. He didn't know what had caused him to fall down the rabbit hole of fear, but he was unable to get out and needed suggestions to help.

If you are like my friend and gripped with fear, read on. There is hope.

Remember, fear is a choice, as is faith. It's also a muscle you need to work in order to mentally be in peak condition. It doesn't come immediately, but over time. If you are looking for a quick fix to get your head straight while you gather your faith then read on, because you are in luck.

The foundation for overcoming fear and living in faith is gratitude. It's that simple. Starting with gratitude and what you are truly thankful for sets you on a path of faith. Try focusing on what you are truly grateful for while holding onto your fear. It won't leave immediately, but it will leave. Darkness cannot live where light resides.

Once you have gratitude under control, you can start to build your faith-based muscle. Prepare to dig in and face your fear with faith. Following this gradually allowed me to pivot to positivity and can help you as well.

Embrace Fear

Although fear isn't real, embrace it as being a part of how we make decisions. Turning thoughts of fear into an awareness of potential danger while attacking with faith takes time. There's no need to ignore your current fear-based life. Instead you should realize and recognize it for what it is—your imagination choosing impending doom as the outcome and not impending BOOM! Recognizing fear allows you to address it, and over time the gap of switching from fear to faith will shorten and your mindset will improve.

Have a Plan

As with anything worthwhile, you need to know where you are going. Planning out what you need to accomplish and the issue causing you fear will help you to see wins and pitfalls. You will know that when things go as planned, even when the plan is hard, you are on the right path. Part of any plan I create is the potential that it will go wrong. It's the contingency plan. And as anyone who's ever taken a breath of life will tell you, things never go entirely according to plan. In heightened emotional states such as fear, consider in advance how you will feel if your plan doesn't go as planned. How will you address fear? For that matter, how will you address wins? Knowing your direction and outcome ahead of time minimizes surprises and the associated fear.

Play the Long Game

Simply put, expect improvements, not perfection. Honing that faith-based muscle takes time and patience.

Act on Your Plan

Action is the key to overcoming fear. Think of it as outrunning the devil. The greater your ability to act is, the more it will allow you to conquer fear. Few things feel better at the end of the day than realizing that you acted and dealt with things instead of ignoring things.

Practice, Exercise, Fail, Repeat

Life is a series of practices, don't expect perfection. Exercise, or do and act, is key as stated. However, know you will fail, we always fail. Take that as a win, you fail and learn, and you got back up and repeated the practice and exercise.

Keep an Eye on Success

Realize that you will have success, some small and some large, and keep your eye out for it. Recognizing your successes provides fuel for your efforts and builds your confidence muscle. Sometimes the success is you made it through the day when you would have rather eaten ice cream and watch YouTube. Confidence builds your faith and stifles fear, success builds confidence.

Communicate with Others

Have a few people to be there to build you up and keep you directionally focused on your plan. They can provide both cheerleading and tough love when needed. Just make sure they have your back regardless.

Be Okay with Failure

Don't be so shocked when you fail. Deal with it. Be okay with failure. Don't expect perfection. Prepare to pick yourself up, dust off and move forward in success.

Stay Positive

Avoid negativity at all costs. That includes not being cynical or petty. Don't talk about others, yourself or anything else negatively. Your thoughts really are things, and the more you realize that and stay positive the greater your faith will be.

Pivot as Needed

Realize that your plan may need adjusting and pivot as needed to reach your goal. The need to pivot may be seen as a failure but it's not. It's part of any good pre-plan preparation. Part of your plan should include when to pivot.

The Glory of Faith

Mastering faith means you are overcoming fear. Remember, however, that it's a process and it takes time. The win is when you truly live in faith, with very minimal fear that's squashed quickly. You'll learn that you can conquer anything. With faith you are prepared to persevere in any situation you choose.

Pills

1. Each time you are faced with fear, catch yourself and ask, can I choose being faithful? Visualize two paths, one leading to fear and one to faith. Remember, you have to choose a path.
2. Remember that even the Magic 8 Ball of faith has twice as many positive affirmations than negative ones. Visualize the positive thoughts when facing fear based ones. Make a conscious effort to choose faith.
3. Practice choosing faith over fear as an exercise. Remember you will fail. Be okay with failing, just remember that you practice, exercise, fail and repeat. Always repeat the practice and exercise.

21 FAILURE AS AN OPTION

"Failure is not an option", a phrase attributed to Gene Kranz, the flight director of the Gemini, Apollo and Space Shuttle missions, is simultaneously both a correct and incorrect statement. We have all heard that, and the majority of us view failure negatively. That's because failure is negative, but it can also be positive. It's for this reason we have difficulty managing the emotions and experiences around failure. We come up with cool sayings like, "It's only failure if you don't get back up and try again." Which again, is both true and untrue.

Let's be honest about failure. First of all, it sucks. We're not talking about inconveniences that could be deemed as failure. We're talking about failure that derails our progress. It just sucks. Secondly, failure in hindsight is redeeming. We can look back, see the obstacles we have overcome, and take pride in our accomplishments. At that point we can actually call failure glorious. So, you see, failure is both a positive and a negative; it both sucks and it is glorious. If failure was a relationship our Facebook status would state, "It's complicated."

This creates a question: how do you know if it's positive or negative? Well, by knowing where you are going. It's that simple. If you don't know where you are going, your view of whether it's positive or negative has minimal value. In fact, if you don't know where you are going then failure or success is a game of chance. To truly embrace the suck and enjoy the glory you need a plan; one that's detailed enough that you can clearly see your direction and vision as you push through. You need to see the end from the beginning. Clarity will help you understand your failure, and ultimately your success.

Failure is Not an Option

Once you've created your plan and it's clearly defined and visible in your mind, be prepared to pivot as needed. Rarely does your defined plan and vision play out exactly as planned—in fact, it almost never will. Pivoting allows you to manage failure as an opportunity to grow, change and learn. Staying on plan does as well, as long as you're not rigid with it. As long as the plan is good, you pivot as needed, and you stay persistent throughout, failure is not an option.

To contradict myself, a plan can fail and often will, so it is an option. Where failure is an option is when you decide to give in, don't create a new plan and go watch TV for the next 30 years.

But you can't quit. Failure is not an option because you are committed to your success. Even when one plan fails, another plan is created. That becomes the ultimate pivot. You won't quit, so you never hit the big, final failure.

Failure is an Option

Even though we know we're not perfect, when we fail at achieving it, we're shocked. We're all guilty of it. Again, failure sucks. However, you have to know you're going to fail, and sometimes those failures are going to be massive. That doesn't make it easy, but we need to allow it to happen and embrace these failures as they come, even when they're massive and hard to handle. I would miss a debt repayment, have to listen to people squeal like pigs, and as hard as that was at times, I knew my success. I was on a journey that, once completed, would be something few people have the stomach to do. That fueled me to see what could be viewed as a massive failure as an inconvenience instead. It felt like failure because I had let people down, and the plan wasn't playing out exactly as laid out.

It was a point of pivot. Time to regroup and reset and get back to working on the plan. Those failures along the way hurt, and in the moment they felt like mountains. Failure is an option, so train yourself to not be overly dramatic when it happens. Manage it, handle it, pivot as needed and get back to action.

Taking Action

Action makes you stronger and larger, while inaction makes you weaker and smaller. The natural inclination we have when we fail is to shrink; to take a step back and doubt ourselves. So, your new goal is to stop doing this. You want to cut down on the time you spend nursing the wounds of failure, because the longer you spend on this, the greater the distance grows between you and your success. When you take a two-day break in recovery you don't just lose two days, you lose momentum. It's a much greater loss than just the days off in failure ICU.

The best thing you can do after a failure is keep moving forward, even if you don't feel 100%. Action creates confidence, gives you purpose, and keeps your momentum going. The only time you should take between a failure and action is how long it takes to review your plan and decide if you need to pivot or not. Remember, take time to ponder the success you created and the end goal. Put your current failure into perspective and feel the growth and success that can come of it. Then, get back to work!

Believe in Yourself

A few months ago, my wife and I were both feeling pretty beat up—I can't remember why, but I remember the event and the emotions. I asked her, how likely it was that she would fail in terms of a percentage. She said 80%, maybe 90%. Then I asked what the likelihood of her completely failing was, and she said 0%. I felt the same way. In the moment we were emotional and had overstated the severity of our problem. When looking long term, we could be logical and realize that we would not fail. We immediately stopped our pity parties and got back to work.

Do you believe in yourself? You either do or you don't, and that has nothing to do with failure. If you don't, you need to find that faith in yourself. If you do, you need to be grounded in that belief and hold onto that knowledge. When you fail, ask the logical question, do I believe in myself? Am I going to succeed or fail long term? Logically, you know you will succeed, so start believing that you will.

Stubbornly Persistent

The definition of persistence is: firm or obstinate continuance in a course of action in spite of difficulty or opposition. Stubborn is to have a dogged determination. Few people truly have a stubborn persistence. Can you look at a situation or at others and say, "If nothing else, I will outlast the situation and everyone else?"

You need to know, deep down, that you will outlast anything and everything. When you do say this enough you build that muscle. You just know. You know that when others say they stay with something you think, "Yeah, sure, you will be long gone when I'm still digging in." It's that level of dogged determination that will get you past your failures quickly.

Blame

You created the problem, so you have to own the problem. Ownership of your failure is liberating, while blaming others makes you a victim. But you are not a victim, you are powerful. You are formidable. You don't blame others for anything, because to do so would admit you gave them your power. This is said in love, not judgement, because as the writer I deeply care about you.

Caring What Others Think

Often, I hear from someone that another person said such and such about them or that they don't like them. This tells me that someone has gotten into their head. I had someone like that in my life, and had they not been a family member, I would have cut them out of my life. When I found myself with her in my head, I started asking myself if she was a VIP? If not, she was not allowed inside the red velvet rope. It did the job, it helped me put her and those thoughts where they needed to be—out of my mind.

How many people who have accomplished a high level of success have bothered to tell you what to do? I would venture none. The only thing opinionated people have perfected and accomplished in life is the ability to craft a well thought out opinion, sprinkled with judgement. Move on; you don't need to spend valuable time caring about what they think.

Goals and End Game

As mentioned, keep the end in sight. Knowing where you're going, what success looks like and holding onto that vision will allow you to pull up that visual, believe it and move forward. Have a plan with clearly defined objectives. Both they and your vision will propel you forward when you need it most.

Remember Gratitude

The importance of gratitude cannot be overstated. Work to have it in your heart and make it something you feel continually. Gratitude makes all your problems smaller. When things go wrong, ask yourself what you're grateful for. You won't want to do it because it interrupts your pity party, but ask yourself what ten things are you grateful for. Get in the habit of gravitating to gratitude for everything. This is an elixir of life. Scripture tells us to pray always. Add gratitude to that. If you are grateful, you will not fail.

Pills

1. When you fail, you need to stop and remember that you believe in yourself. Logically, you know you can accomplish what you need to do.
2. When you fail you must take action quickly. Do not revert to wallowing; move quickly to reset and get your momentum back.
3. Always be grateful, whether times are good or bad.
4. Determine right now, right here, that you will be stubbornly persistent. Make that pledge to yourself.

22 DETERMINING WHAT YOU WANT TO ACHIEVE

I was so busy working, building and developing the company that it wasn't until things broke down that I started to take a deeper look at what I wanted. Once I knew I was determined to keep the company alive and rebuild it, I turned to a deeper question. What was it that I wanted to achieve? My identity was so tied to the company that when it ebbed and flowed I did as well. I had to break away and think about what I wanted for myself. The company was on its path to health and sustainability, but what about me?

There wasn't an easy answer. It definitely wasn't bailing out a company that was taking on water, bailing quicker and quicker as more water came in. That was what I needed to do, but it wasn't what I wanted to achieve.

I wanted so much more.

Pull Yourself Up

At some level, you have now reached the point where you need to determine what you want to achieve because things aren't going as designed. You want more but realize that what you have been doing isn't providing what you need creatively, emotionally, financially or in some other way. You are at a crossroads and need to determine where you go next. Be positive—this is the beginning of the next phase of your life! That attitude will get you a lot further a lot faster, and with greater clarity than focusing on the potential need to start over again.

Personally, that meant re-evaluating what I wanted my role in my company to be, what else I wanted to do in life, and how I might achieve all of it simultaneously. It was an adventure.

Take Your Time

There's no rush. We often feel like we need to pivot quickly, make a change and determine the next steps now. We don't. We have time, so use it. Nothing could be worse than rushing the decision, only to realize you've made the wrong call. We all know people that one day are doing this thing, the next they are onto that. They can't gravitate and stick to something. Don't be like them.

For me, that meant analyzing and growing into the next phase of my life over a three-year period. There was no rush. I had my company to fix, and that was my main priority. I had plenty of time to contemplate my next move.

Don't Stop What You're Doing Now

Chances are that you are not in a place financially where you can stop everything, shift and move into what you truly want to achieve. Don't make the mistake of abandoning what you have now for what you want in the future. Instead, make what you have now work and accomplish what you need while you prepare to make your next move. You may be able to close up what you are doing now in a matter of weeks; you may be able to find a new job quickly and give notice to your business or employer. Most of us, however, need to have things in order before we move onto our next great thing. That takes as long as it takes. It's unique to everyone—for some, it's closing a door on the past, while for others it's preparing it for someone else to manage so you can move onto your next achievement.

I needed to get the company's finances in order and get it back on a solid foundation. However, I knew that in the long term I would set myself up to be an advisor to the company and not involved in the day to day activities. That is still an action plan, not a reality. The shift is happening where I won't be the CEO and I'll focus on sales. Then, the shift will be for me to hand the sales off and focus on advising the company and growing my next business venture. That venture has started to take shape because of this book. Not stopping what I'm doing will allow me to live in fullness and enjoy my current company as an advisor and grow something new.

Life is meant to be a joyous adventure, so live it that way!

Keep What's Working

Take time and review what's working in your life and career. There are many things you are probably very good at, and those are the areas you can build around. Often, when reconsidering where you are at and what you want to achieve, people focus on the new and exciting. But the old is what's worked, and it's a great place to build your new and exciting venture. Not everything that's led you to revisit and revise your career was bad, there's a lot that was good.

That can and should be where you build your foundation.

One amazing advantage I have now is the leadership and management skills gained, and my ability to dig in and complete any task. I can focus and complete like never before. These are just a few of the many areas where I can build foundations for the future. Why would I consider throwing that out?

Regret Nothing

There are few things that will serve you less and cause you more problems in life than living with regrets. Regrets are sneaky; they creep into your thoughts and fester. Unless you manage them, they will get squatter rights. They absolutely do not serve you.

Talk to yourself as if you are speaking to another person. You would tell them that self-hatred isn't serving them. You would ask how those thoughts are affecting their actions and behavior. You may ask them how they are benefiting from the self-hatred.

I've previously mentioned the deep regret I had when I found out that my company was in trouble; my regret that I had caused it and that I had made so many poor choices. I can't clearly state how deep that regret was. I sat for weeks just staring out in my own misery, only leaving to go to the office. My evenings and weekends were reserved for deep regret and pity. Today, after living through that, I can honestly say I have a deep level of gratitude for that experience. I remember that guy and I know I'll never go back there. I plan to have few regrets in life. If something doesn't serve us, we should eliminate it as quickly as possible.

Be Selfish

Determining what you want to achieve will require a certain level of selfishness. The idea of taking care of number one doesn't sit well with many, but making sure that your needs are met and knowing what you want to achieve will help you define your direction. Remember, this is what you want to achieve, not what others want you to achieve. This means that at times, you will need to be selfish with your time and resources. When you set down timelines, as an example, you need to guard that and not allow a time thief to come in and take them from you.

There were many ways I chose to be selfish while improving the state of my business. I learned to be more selfish when I opted to pay myself before paying down a debt. I learned to be more selfish when I was telling people I didn't have time to socialize. Taking time for myself ultimately allowed me to give back. Had I not taken some money before paying others back there was a high chance no one would get anything. It's also extremely empowering to say and do something for yourself.

Figure Out What You Need

There's always time to look at what you need—indeed, perhaps there is no better time than when you have experienced a life altering moment. It's good to take time alone to ponder and reflect on what's most important. How quickly do you want to dive into something new? Do you want to stay doing what you are doing, but with necessary alterations? How does a change affect your family? What will it do to your finances, positively or negatively? Rushing into a new venture is like leaving a bad relationship and jumping immediately into a new one. It may or may not be good, but taking the time to think improves the likelihood the results will meet what you both need and want.

Spending time on what I needed became a regular activity. There were so many moving parts that I often questioned what I needed and wanted. This propelled me into moving in the direction that best fit my personal objectives around my company. At times, I had to do something that didn't match what I needed personally. But asking that question helped prioritize the activity and minimize the time spent on it. My ongoing objective now is to determine what I need and then gravitate toward that.

What Makes Me Happy?

I'm not a big proponent of the theory that you should create a business around what you love and what makes you happy. When I hear that my first thought is, if there's no money in it, then what makes you happy will soon make you unhappy. However, there are things that make you happy that you can leverage into your next venture. Do people make you happy? If so, you may not want to train to be a software developer that has little interaction with others. Alternatively, do you find your true happiness by being alone? Then consider things where you can create as a solo contributor with minimal exposure to others. Happiness needs to be built into anything you do; it needs to bring you joy.

Through my troubles, I discovered that I really loved helping others. I had no idea that service to others was service to me. Now, future ventures will always include a component of helping others succeed.

Enlist Others to Help You

You are never going to reach your new venture without the help of others. We are all a sum of those we surround ourselves with, which makes it incredibly important for us to align ourselves with the highest quality people. Your network is powerful. If it's not, set out to find great people and mentors to help you where you need to go. Those people need your power as much as you need theirs. It should be a mutually beneficial, and ideally long-term arrangement. They will be loyal and admire and appreciate who you are and what you intend to accomplish. Enlist those individuals regularly, and they will be excited to help.

I have a few individuals that I'm extremely close to. They know what

I aim to accomplish, and they check in with me to hear what my objectives are for the week and how well I'm staying on task. I'll stay up late working on things just so I don't have to hear them beat on me for missing deadlines. In turn, I do the same for them. They are true friends and allies. I can't fail because they won't allow it. They hold me accountable.

Stay Positive

It's easy to get off the rails and lose your focus when you start something new. There are competing needs, from current work requirements to personal activities, and it's easy for the new and developing venture to take a backseat at times. Things may not progress or develop at the rate you would like. Stay positive and remember the path you are on. Staying positive combats any regrets that come up, just as the regrets combat any positive momentum. Expressing gratitude and serving others are great ways to improve your mood and will help you stay positive.

This hasn't always been easy for me, which is why mentioning this is important to me. I want to impart upon you how deeply staying positive can improve your efforts and actions, not just your mood. It's a constant work in progress for me, but as I practice and live in awareness I'm able to see all the beauty that surrounds me, the flowing opportunities and all the other advantages the world has for people willing to make the effort. Knowing this provokes gratitude in me and allows me to stay positive.

Don't Procrastinate

Let's be very clear: procrastination stands between you and your success and vision. Procrastination is sneaky. It allows you to feel you are not really putting something off, but merely delaying it momentarily. You know it needs to be done, but something else important came up. But there will always be things that come up. The next thing will fill the void of the last thing that just left, and it'll push your new venture off further. Set goals, assign dates and stick to them. If they slip because you underestimated the depth of time it would take that's one thing, but if it slips because you procrastinate that's another. Procrastination is like a dripping faucet, it's slow and consistent. It builds over time and soon you've lost years.

Early on, writing this book was a textbook example of what I just mentioned. I set a plan, missed it and reset only to miss it again. Finally, I set real goals on what I wanted to accomplish and put my network of friends on notice that I needed them to help keep me from procrastinating. If this was as important to me as I said it was, I needed to treat it like I do those things that are truly important in my life. Procrastination ended; this book will be done on schedule. Feel free to ask me if it was done as designed or if this is a total crap section of the book. You are now part of my network, so hold me accountable as I hold you.

Get Excited, Possibilities Abound

You should be excited, full of high-octane output ready to slay the possibilities in front of you. It should be easy to look backwards on your regrets and short comings, where you failed and how you didn't measure up. Alternatively, look forward with excitement about where you are going and how the lessons learned will catapult you to superstardom. The quicker you get your head in the game and start to move forward, the better this adventure will be. You are about to embark on an adventure, you just need to determine if it's one full of excitement or regret.

Pills

1. Take time to understand where you are right now. Contemplate, and don't rush into a decision. Weigh your options and discuss with a mentor. Once you have your answer, determine your actions and your plan.

2. Get excited about the plan, about the possibilities and opportunities. Do not focus on what could have been, focus on what will be. Regret nothing.
3. Determine what makes you happy. Focus and gravitate to those things that bring joy and happiness.
4. Do not procrastinate. Everyday take stock of what you are doing and evaluate whether you are procrastinating or actively moving things forward.

23 ELIMINATE THE UNNECESSARY AND AVOID AT ALL COSTS

The level of unnecessary activities faced each day is daunting. When time isn't critical this goes unnoticed, but when time is critical this is front and center. These activities are your time wasters and energy suckers.

In one week, my life switched. I was busy moving forward in my business making seemingly great progress and growth. Our revenue was at an all-time high. When it all broke open and reality set in, tasks that seemed harmless and that I'd paid no attention to became hyper visible and costly. The unnecessary is always costly, just not always seen.

One day I sat with my VP of Operations and we estimated that 40% of a given week was spent talking about debt, creditors, repayment, cash flow or anything that kept the balls we were juggling from hitting the ground. I remember asking him if we really had to do all this and if we had to be reactionary. I wanted to know if it could wait, and if someone else could handle things so I could focus on other areas. These conversations were difficult, but they started us on the path to eliminating unnecessary activities and avoiding them at all costs.

Why the Need to Eliminate

Life is full of activities that you are faced with daily. At work you have meetings, emails, and phone calls, while personally there's the need for housework, looking after the dog and more. Those things that enter our lives can come unannounced and unplanned, and we often turn to work on them because they will only take a few minutes.

Have you ever worked and worked and worked all day, only to feel like you haven't accomplished anything? It's not that you haven't accomplished anything—it's that you haven't accomplished anything important. The need to eliminate comes from our need to accomplish. At times we need to be misers with our time, telling people and tasks that we don't have time today. We do this, because otherwise, we end up questioning why we haven't gotten anything done. At home, not focusing on the important and eliminating the intrusions may be an inconvenience. The grass is a day longer and the car a little dirtier. In business it's much more than an inconvenience, it's essential that you eliminate the unnecessary so you can meet corporate objectives. If your business is struggling, it's imperative that you eliminate and reassign as quickly as possible. That's where we were.

Our greatest need was to drive revenue, increase sales, get money in and pay down debt. Talking about debt, speaking to creditors and giving attention to those and other needless areas needed to be eliminated. Interestingly, two of us were covering what could have been done by one. However, we found ourselves reacting to requests from others, huddling in a meeting discussing how we would respond and then springing into a response. Fortunately, this activity didn't last long before we started asking the obvious question—why were we doing this?

Simplifying Your Life

What does your perfect day look like? When the day is done, what will provide you with a sense of accomplishment? Questions like these will allow you to outline your days. There are only so many things you can accomplish in a day, and when you realize that many of them will take deep thought or extended time periods you find there are only a few things to focus on.

The first step in simplifying is by minimizing. Do this by determining the few and most critical opportunities facing you each day. These should be things that move you forward in the short and long term. They shouldn't be tasks that include putting the garbage out because it's Thursday. In addition to those few essential items, look to add things that need to be done but can be accomplished quickly. This could be a series of important emails that need responses, an employee issue or a brief meeting. Think of these as items that can be bundled into thirty-minute blocks. You want to leave most of your time for the essential large opportunities.

For me, this meant a thirty-minute burst of email requests, discussions about debt that needed my attention or other items. The rest of the time was spent on clients and potential clients. It was all about driving revenue.

Look to prioritize productivity over busy work. As an example, when I have an essential opportunity to find a new client I will say "Find one new potential to add to the sales pipeline." I avoid saying, "Spend two hours contacting new clients." One is specific; finding a new opportunity to add to the sales pipeline. The other is vague, other than two hours, which could easily be interrupted or spent doing busy, unproductive preparation instead of finding new clients.

One last point for simplifying: focus on prioritizing your work. Out of your essentials, which is the most critical? That's where you start. Often, people focus on what's easy, more interesting or can be done quickly when they should be focusing on the most important. The only caveat to that is the thirty-minute burst of work that can be bundled together.

Eliminating the Unneeded

We should never assume that just because someone asks us to do something, we need to do it. We should continually ask ourselves if the task is needed in order to reach our largest objectives. When you look out the window and see the lawn needs mowed, that doesn't mean you need to mow it right now. In business, just because someone sends you an email requesting something important to them it doesn't mean that it's important or needful for you. Your goal is to provide clarity. Elimination does this and frees up your time.

Delegate, Delegate, Delegate

In the above analogy of the lawn needing mowing, just because it's needed doesn't mean you need to do it. Your objective is to create time to do the highest essential items, create clarity and move the large rocks forward. In business many things can be handled by others. If you are a small business owner, outsource your taxes, janitorial services or other non-essential tasks. If your business is larger, hand off non-essential tasks to an assistant. All too often, I see people doing things because it's quicker to do it themselves than to have someone else do it. Except that one thing is multiplied by all the meaningless tasks of the day and it carves into the time needed for your essential few. Get in the habit of asking yourself if a task can be delegated. If it can be, it should be.

Simplify Where You Will Commit

How much can you really do? Where can you eliminate? You may see yourself as superhuman, able to accomplish more than the average human, and who knows, you could even be correct. Alternatively, you may be the type of person that doesn't like to say no to others. But even superhumans need to simplify so they can accomplish their essential few tasks, even if this is three to four tasks and not two to three like us mere mortals. If you tend to say yes because you don't like to disappoint others, we are going to help you here too. In both cases, you need to learn to say no. Your time is valuable, so treat it like it is.

This starts with being honest with yourself and others. This means you need to pause and consider how simplifying your commitments will actually allow you to grow and advance. Likewise, when dealing with time sucking individuals, you should pause and consider simplifying your commitments. Once you've done that, the answer should often be, "No, unfortunately I can't take on more." You will disappoint, but over time others will stop asking and you will learn that focusing on the essential tasks takes your superhuman abilities to ultra-superhuman.

Track Your Necessary to Eliminate the Unnecessary

Consider using the Opportunity Pipeline mentioned in the book to help you focus on the necessary and to eliminate the unnecessary. This will give you a vision into your possibilities and then drive them down into an annual overview that you can monitor to meet monthly, weekly, daily and even hourly opportunities. You should monitor and track to stay on course for the essential few.

Things to Consider

Think of why you need to eliminate the unnecessary. We live in an age where there are constant distractions—from our smartphone apps, social media, messaging and contact methods such as phones and email. As I write I sit in a hotel lobby, two TVs with the sound up, music and people walking around in various conversations, all fighting equally for my attention. The unnecessary is all around us. The need to gain clarity is ever-increasing in our lives. The more we can pinpoint this focus, the greater our clarity becomes and the more important work we can do. Then, if you really want, you will have free time to enjoy a distraction on your terms.

Pills

1. Take a moment and consider what you can eliminate from your life. What tasks are you doing that you don't need to? Concentrate on gaining time to do more of what needs to be done.
2. What can you delegate? Can someone else take some of your workload? Consider all the ways you can potentially delegate and then start to do this.
3. What ways can you simplify your life? Can you eliminate your day down to the critical tasks that move you forward in big ways? Can you block time out for the trivial and only do these tasks then? Your goal is to not get easily distracted.

24 REINVENTING YOURSELF AND YOUR BUSINESS AFTER FAILURE

You've had the epiphany, the realization that your business is in severe and potentially catastrophic trouble. You are now at the first of many crossroads. Do you continue in your business and right the wrongs or do you quit and start over?

Unfortunately, it is not as simple as picking one and finding freedom and peace. Both will be difficult, laden with thoughts that there must be an easier way. When these moments arise, consider choosing the smarter way over the seemingly easier path.

The Case for Hardship

The path of least resistance is alluring. It takes us back to a level of comfort we're familiar with and have become accustomed to enjoying. Alternatively, the path of endurance slowly takes us to a new place of growth, wisdom, skills and accomplishment. Simply, do we choose the front-end, easier path or the back-end, value path?

Enduring through a rebuild shows our willingness to keep a promise to ourselves to stay with something, no matter what. It means we don't quit because difficulties come our way, severe as they may be. Conversely, deciding to take the easy path may mean our failure to endure when hard things come our way. if we take this path, we are consciously making the decision to back away from the business we started and believed in.

There are times when the smart decision is to close our doors and move onto our next great venture. Perhaps the product we developed doesn't have a market, we face a rebuild with a bad product or a restart with a new idea. Choosing a path that's hard because we've put so much emotion, time and money into our business only to realize we need to move on is a legitimate decision. That's also a case for hardship, to endure through a new process and to take the best of the old and to add that the best of the new.

Move Toward Risks

When we find ourselves rebuilding, it's likely that we are close to tapped out in the business. We could be in emotional, financial or spiritual debt. These feelings often leave us polarized, unable to move in any direction. Perhaps we are emotionally tapped out, or unsure what to do next. We can feel vulnerable and weak, unworthy of doing what we need to do. Ironically, this is the time when you should be strong and willing to fail even more. It was risk that got us into the situation we are in. When we should have been more calculated and cautious, we acted risky. Now we need to rebuild, and we are risk averse. That's backwards. When I realize the depth of my corporate debt I sunk into depression, questioning every decision I had to make moving forward. What I ultimately learned was that because my personal and business finances were shot, I could continue to take risks because I had nothing to lose. Being at rock bottom gave me the courage to take necessary and smart risks. When we find ourselves in a rebuild, we're in the perfect place to take smart and calculated risks.

Setting the Stage for Your Reinvention

Failure is a blessing. Instead of asking why me, ask why not me? We should be grateful for the position we find ourselves in. We face another crossroad—the decision to wallow and lament, or to show gratitude for the opportunity that failure has placed in our life. Either way, here we are. We either restart with wallow or restart with gratitude, but we are restarting. Look at failure as a blessing, not a curse.

This reboot comes with knowledge we have gained. We need to put our ego in check, believe in ourselves and dig in, create a great plan, act and prepare to conquer. We need to start picking the sword up in strength, instead of dragging it into battle in weakness.

Keys to Reinventing Yourself and Your Business

Mindset

The depth at which our thoughts matter can't be covered adequately here, but here lies the key to all our success or lack of success. Everything comes down to our thoughts. They determine our outcome. It's both as simple and as complicated as that. This is incredibly deep when it comes to all areas of life, and specifically for a rebuild, when things are in an emotional flux, the need for proper thought is critical. Our mindset should control all aspects of what we do. Consider what we say about ourselves, others, situations and everything else. Get your thoughts set and the rest will fall into place.

Business is Saturated

Often, I hear people say that you should find a market that's untapped and go after that. I just typed in untappedbusiness.com and the URL is for sale—there isn't even a market for a domain name to cover an unsaturated market. There are always plenty of companies selling and doing what you are doing. I hear people talk about how I'm in the booming business of cyber security, that there must be tons of opportunities—and there are, but there is also a lot of competition. The combination of saturated markets and a need to drive revenue to solve our problems may push us to consider lowering our prices or giving deep discounts. This knee jerk reaction comes from scarcity and fear, but it's not a sustainable long-term strategy. Lowering our pricing aligns us with lower level clients and puts us in competition with lower level competitors. Thus, it makes us a lower level company. We need to focus on value as a strategy, and build on differentiating ourselves for quality and service, not price. Ours should be a long-term strategy of growth as we reinvent.

Focus on Your Ideal Client

Cash is king, revenue is critical, so the temptation is there to take money and clients as they come. Money is money, right?

Wrong.

Recently, we took on a project that was just outside our skillset, but within our area of experience. This was a risk. After all, we just discussed risk as good right? We spoke of calculated risk with a high reward. We discovered as we moved deeper into this project that the skills required were further outside the skillset of my team than we originally thought. In order to deliver on the project, we needed to hire a subcontractor to push this through to completion. Ultimately, the client received what they wanted and at best we broke even financially. I learned from this that we must define what our ideal client looks like and stay focused on them.

Don't Expect an Overnight Fix

Something I've learned over the years is that whatever I need to do, I should expect it to take three times longer than I originally planned. My initial thinking was that we could get through our financial troubles at my company in a year, and instead it took us three. People tend to assume they can accomplish things much quicker than they can. This causes anxiety and frustration as the expectation versus the reality sets in. Figure out a conservative timetable to fix your troubles, then play it safe and multiply it by three. Having the expectation that it will take longer prepares you for the reality of the long-haul. If it turns out you can get it done in a third of the time, congratulations! You've accomplished a great feat.

Be Consistent

Before I mastered delegating tasks to others, as a small business owner I tended to do too much. I handled project management, vendor management, dabbled with the debt repayment, met with employees or did what I felt needed to be done. Jumping from one task to the other caused erratic and inconsistent behavior and results. This hit our sales hardest. I focused on selling, and then when the pipeline got full and the projects came in, I shifted more to project management, recruiting, employee management and several things that took my foot off the gas. In turn, the pipeline opportunities would get stale, new opportunities wouldn't be added, and ultimately the sales engine would start back up to refill the pipeline and close more projects. The inconsistent process would rinse and repeat, and every time we had to find our momentum again.

Reinvention of your business will require you to be consistent and to put the most important things first. Your company's primary objective is to drive revenue. If you're in reinvention or salvage mode that need is magnified. If that's your strong suit, then consistently focus in that area. If not, find someone who can consistently deliver for you. It starts with consistent sales and is followed by the need to consistently deliver on your promises in all areas of your business.

Enjoy the Journey

Few things caused me more hell and joy than those three years, to the point I often wondered if I was bipolar. I had up and down mood swings, depending on the day, hour or new information and a host of influences that caused my emotions to ebb and flow. It wasn't until I was able to see what I was doing as truly a rare and unique experience that I realized I was on a journey. I now look back at it with fondness. I don't miss it and I hope to never experience anything like that again, but nothing could have created the person I am today more thoroughly than that mess. At the time I saw how weak I was, and all I wanted was to curl up in the fetal position and rock myself to sleep. But I didn't; I handled the problems and I got better with each passing day. I now feel formidable and capable of handling anything. I just wish I would have enjoyed the journey more. I write this with no pearls of wisdom for you on how to do that in the moment, other than realize that you are capable and will come out with strength you've never dreamed of. At the end of this journey you will look back and think, "Holy crap, I did that!"

Pills

1. Can you logically make a case for yourself to embrace hardship? Can you see the result from where you are now? Can you feel the growth, wisdom, skills and a sense of accomplishment that will come from persevering?
2. What areas can you move toward risks? Can you logically consider and act upon calculated risks?
3. Can you set the stage for what you are embarking upon as a blessing? Can you say, why not me?

4. Where can you integrate the keys to reinventing you into your plan? Which of those will you start with first?

25 STAY TRUE TO YOUR RESOLVE – STAYING IN ALIGNMENT

In the "Autobiography of Benjamin Franklin" he provides a list of thirteen virtues, one of which covers resolve: "Resolve to perform what you ought; perform without fail what you resolve." To resolve means to have a firm decision, to be committed, determined and to be decisive. The person we wish to be tomorrow comes from the commitment we have today to act with resolve.

What is Resolve?

Resolve is our ability to see something, know what we want to accomplish and then to stick with it through all the hardships, ups and downs, distractions, naysayers and everything else that comes your way. To have true resolve you know the end result and will do everything in your power to reach it. Resolve is a great compass that keeps us committed and focused on staying our course. Resolve makes us put aside wants, needs, desires and all things that cross our path in reaching our desired goal. With resolve, we know that the only thing that stands between us and our end result is time and the obstacles we will overcome. With deep resolve, you know it's merely a matter of time.

Finding Our Resolve

In 1978 Michael Jordan, arguably the best basketball player in history, found himself on the outside of his high school varsity team looking in. He was a Sophomore who had seen a fellow Sophomore make the varsity squad while he was moved to the JV roster. Upon seeing this, Jordan went home and cried in his room. It was that moment where Jordan found his deep resolve to become the greatest in the world. His resolve was so strong and so deeply committed that he was known to be overbearing to teammates, opposing players and anything that would stand in his way of his resolve to be the best.

Resolve isn't an intellectual process. Yes, you must be intelligent with what you do, but you can't just say you're going to have resolve and then set out on your directed path. However, there is a moment, or series of moments in your life where something is activated, and the switch happens. Resolve is that part of you deep inside that says, "This is what needs to be done and I will do everything and anything to make it a reality." It's that moment when you say, enough. Enough average. Enough waiting. Enough of what other people think. Enough of thinking small. You think, I've had enough and anyone and anything that gets in the way of my resolve will meet an immovable force. Resolve isn't fleeting, it is always seeking and finding more sources of energy it can sap to grow bigger, stronger and deeper.

Losing Our Resolve

Although resolve isn't fleeting and is always seeking a power source, it's just like anything else. Without that power source, it diminishes over time. For Michael Jordan, it would have looked like letting up a little on his practicing or taking a little rest. Then, a little more. Then, seeing another player outplay him and commenting, "This isn't fair, I have more talent than that guy."

When we choose to let off the proverbial gas pedal and our resolve slows, we weaken ourselves. Then, because we know the resolve we had, we find ourselves a victim lashing out. We blame others, criticize them, judge them, and make excuses why they stood in our way and made our success impossible. But deep down, we know that we should be lashing out at ourselves. The victim we are is the victim we allowed to grow within us. That blame, criticism and judgement should be placed upon our shoulders.

Guard your resolve and feed its fuel. It's easier to maintain a healthy fire than it is to go out in search of what we need to start a new one.

Fueling Your Resolve

You care deeply about your goals, vision and direction. Could you imagine Michael Jordan half-heartedly committing to his excellence? The passion and resolve you have for your goals impacts how successful you will be. This will propel you to wake early, work through lunch, work late into the night and to do all those things you've been told attribute to an unhealthy lifestyle. Your resolve and your goals supersede logic. Your resolve will push your vision and goals into reality.

Endurance is your friend. You see your daily failures, large and small, as obstacles on the path to your success. You know you will be knocked down repeatedly—and every time you'll get up again. When others say, "Enough is enough" you say, "I have one more in me, so let's do this." You always have one more in you. You have a deep-seated belief that the more you do, the more that happens because of you. You overcome, and that's the added fuel that you need to keep your fire burning. Your fire gets drained with each obstacle encounter, but with each obstacle you overcome, you've added more fuel than you took. You know that endurance is the fuel that grows your resolve.

The odds are against you. Don't think so? Look around and listen—no doubt there are people all around you willing to tell you why you can't do something. Of course, they're experts in underachieving and know exactly what that looks like. People that have actually done something will cheer you on from the mountain top, while those in the valley will tell you to stay there where it's comfortable.

But that's just the listening part. Look around and you will see the odds are against you, because there are so few people on the mountain tops and the valley is littered with people who never succeeded. However, you have resolve, so ignore the odds and the people. When they say it can't be done, you agree with them—for them, it can't. But for you, you know its only time and overcoming obstacles that stand between you and those on the mountain top. Each naysayer doesn't sap your fuel, but they pile fuel upon you. Because you know that someday you won't need to say, "I told you I could do it" because they will see your success as proof you were right.

Staying in Alignment

Each day you will be faced with the opportunity to tackle the obstacles and strengthen your resolve or to let up, take it easy and let off the gas. You want to stay in alignment with your resolve and goals. But how will you know if you're in or out of alignment? For me, it's simple. At the end of the day, I look at my Opportunity Pipeline and I can see if I've met my daily resolve and if I'm in alignment with what my future holds for me. It really is as simple as that. It's a gut check—do I feel good or is my solar plexus acting up?

Here are some ways that you can take to guide you daily toward staying in alignment with your resolve.

Meditation

Meditation is much more than sitting still. It is a time where you can align yourself with what is of greatest importance for you. For me, that means I take the time to understand God, His thoughts and how my thoughts and desires can align with His and my greatest good. If not God, for you it may be the universe, or it could be yourself. However, meditation is done daily, as often as needed, to center yourself on what you need to accomplish and to stay with your resolve. Think of meditation as an opportunity to wash your car several times a day—whenever it gets dirty you take it through the carwash. Meditation is like a carwash for your mind.

Live in the Moment, Eye to the Future

Staying in alignment means that you understand that in the moment everything is fine. The obstacle you are facing is just a snapshot in time, a bit player in your overall resolve to accomplish your goals. However, while living in the moment you have a clear vision of your future. You understand that what happens today, impacts tomorrow. What happens tomorrow, impacts your lifetime.

Make a Decision on What Truly Matters

There are only a few things in life that truly matter, and those tend to be your family, health, spirituality and finances. Only you can determine what truly matters. Using what truly matters as a stake in the ground allows you to manage your resolve. You manage it by not straying away from what matters most and using this to add fuel to your resolve. Contemplate what matters most daily, and this and your meditation will impact your resolve.

Create and Follow Your Affirmactions

To remind you, an Affirmaction is the ability to take an affirmation and tie it to action. An affirmation is the positive thought and statement you make that something in the future is true. An Affirmaction is taking that affirmation and putting it into action. No affirmation is complete without taking action and having affirmation and action in alignment with your resolve will create the manifestation of your visions and goals.

Use the Opportunity Pipeline

The Opportunity Pipeline is designed to help grow resolve, create momentum and provide you a view on your largest visions in life. Start with what you need to do this year and trickle it down to what you need to do hourly in order to make sure that you stay resolved and manifest those visions into reality.

Use it nightly to outline what you are going to do the following day. When doing so review the, "My Present State" section down through the year, month and week, look at what you're going to accomplish and see what that feels like. Then make sure your opportunities for tomorrow match up with what you need to accomplish for the week.

The more you live the Opportunity Pipeline, the greater your success will be.

Expect Resolve to Work

Is our resolve successful because we declare our thoughts to the universe and good things come back to us, like so many new age authors mention? Or are we successful with resolve because we see success, and success breeds more success? Perhaps it's a combination of the two. I tend to believe that what I state and feel creates a frequency within me that propels things outward, and others notice and feel that. When our frequency is down, people notice that as well. When my frequency is high, things happen for and because of me. The best comes from a combination of putting your thoughts out there to the universe, God or whomever and making your statement of what you want. Then, getting to work with resolve to make sure that happens. This is the best of both—it's sort of hedging our bets.

Saint Augustine said, "Pray as though everything depends on God. Work as though everything depends on you."

From a new age perspective, we're saying, "Put your thought out there to God, the universe or whomever. Declare your intent. Then, get to work and make sure it happens." Regardless of whichever camp you're in, or if you're firmly rooted in both intention and work as I am, expect resolve to work. When we believe in what we're tasking ourselves to do, when we act in resolve and stay in alignment our objectives may not be met as quickly as we would like or plan. However, they will be met. Being resolved means you have created yourself into an unstoppable force. The greatest test of your resolve will be time and patience. With enough of both, you will turn your vision into a manifested reality.

Pills

1. You are embarking on a new path. You need resolve. What resolve do you have? Where can you say, "This is what will happen, and I will not stop until it's completed?"
2. Has something punched you in the gut, where you can hang your determination and resolve to meet your objectives? What is that? Say it out loud in the mirror daily until you feel that burning resolve deeply.
3. How will you implement the steps outlined in the Staying in Alignment section? Where will you start?

26 PUTTING IT ALL TOGETHER FOR SUCCESS

You are one of the few—those who have decided to embrace the hard challenge of taking your business from mess to success. It won't be an easy transition, and it will likely take longer than you anticipate. You will come across bumps, obstacles, doubt, weakness and your own insecurities during the process. But there will be victories as well, those moments that keep your momentum going and your belief growing. You are on your way from being one of the few willing to embark on this challenge, to an even fewer number that take things all the way to success. That's the moment you stand on top of the mountain and look down and see the path taken, the obstacles overcome and the victories you had on your way to that ultimate moment and victory. Soak it in. Not just when you arrive, but right now. Feel what it'll be like when you have accomplished what many said you couldn't. That's a piece of advice I wish I had at the beginning, to feel the win from the start. Go back to it when things got tough, so I could use it as a crutch and motivator to hold me up until I was able to get back to problem solving.

How Will You know When You've Reached Success?

In hindsight, my arrival to success was obvious. It was when we paid off the hard money lender. Why? Because they were the largest debt, the most vocal, and created the highest level of pain and worry for us. You may think it was the IRS, but they worked with us and they are used to reworking payment structures. All the others were a collection of debt with varying levels of noise and complaints, but individually they were harmless to us. When we wired that final payment to the hard money lender, it was a moment we all felt relief. Looking back, I wish we had realized and acknowledge that this final payment to them would be the point we recognized success.

Your success may be attainable by one event, much as ours was, but perhaps it's a series of events that needs to transpire prior to success being declared. Take time to determine when that point is, then gravitate toward that moment. Look at ways to bring that moment around quicker. If, like us, that event will take time, try finding small victories along the way. We could have done this with each payment made, but we chose just to see them as obligations instead. Think about how much better it would have been if we could have gone so far as enjoying the payments! Perhaps that's crazy, but at least we could have seen it as the advancement up the mountain it was.

What's your point of success?

Set Clear Expectations with People

With 18 different individuals and companies owed money, employees that needed to be kept apprised on the status of the company, as well as others like my wife that needed to be kept in the loop there was a lot of expectations. There were also expectations that we had to communicate with ourselves on what we could do and when. There was a constant, seemingly endless need to keep people informed on the status of payments, progress and the health of the organization.

It's a tiring process, and when you must state expectations that aren't favorable to people there's a tendency to fudge reality. Cash flow may show the ability to make payroll over the coming two weeks, but little else. However, there are a few deals in the pipeline that most likely will close which will net you money immediately. The temptation rests with the desire to minimize blowback from people. Consider having to tell everyone it's status quo at least over the next few weeks, which means no payment. You might think that you could tell at least a few that it looks like the money will be available and you could possibly pay them, but you must resist that temptation. Work with actual numbers and communicate factually. It may not seem like you have power, but the truth is that you have all the power. You hold the keys to them getting their money back, with people feeling confident in the future and the overall communication of things. The more you communicate factually, even when it's hard, the increased likelihood you gain respect and keep that power.

Prepare to Miss Those Expectations

One reason to communicate clearly and accurately is that at some point something will spring up that disrupts you. The unforeseen always comes up, and it's exacerbated when things like funds are already razor thin. One small thing can spin everything into a large and arduous ordeal. If you have communicated clearly and accurately, then when the unexpected happens you can go back to those people with a level of credibility. However, each time you go back and state that your intent to act upon what you said isn't going to happen, the more that credibility erodes. You want to minimize this.

We had to clearly and factually state to the hard money lender for roughly two years that we could not pay them. They yelled, screamed, threatened and lied but we held our ground because saying what they wanted to hear was only going to cause greater problems. There were times where we would sit around and try and work things out internally, tempted to compromise with them. But we always found ourselves asking then what? Well, they would expect another payment in a week or two, which we couldn't make. The fact was that we couldn't commit to anything until we could fully commit to everything. When we did come to an agreement on timing, we stated that our expectation was that we would probably be late or miss a payment here or there. Not intentionally, but it was a likelihood. That wasn't well received, but we needed to prepare them for that expectation.

Human nature is to put off pain today for peace, but pushing the pain to tomorrow only increases it and erodes trust. Handling today what should be managed today builds character. Consider character building as the reward for trouble and pain caused you through the ordeal. Doing so somewhat tricks the mind into payments for services rendered.

Managing Emotions

Few things will cause an emotional rollercoaster like having to rebuild your business and knowing that dozens of people are waiting to hear from you, waiting to see if you are good for the money. There may be a combination of that being a reality and it being the mental image you create in the midst of this mental battle you're experiencing.

You sit there working, feeling peace and progress happening and then it happens. The phone rings, an email happens, or a letter in the mail. Something comes in that pushes that rollercoaster down a steep dip until you freefall. You find yourself riding highs and lows, feeling anxiety and looking around every proverbial corner seeing what's next. You ask yourself, "Am I losing my mind?"

Stop. Just stop. Stop letting your thoughts control you. Stop allowing your thoughts to create fictional scenarios. The sooner you can get your head straight and your thoughts right, the quicker you can get the truly necessary things done. At this point in life I can confidently say that both you and I have conquered everything that's come our way. Why? Because here we are, still alive and still moving forward. We have been victorious up to this point, and there is a 100% likelihood that we will continue that way until we leave this earth. We are victorious. We need to start acting like a champion.

Tim Grover said, "Control your thoughts and you'll control your emotions, control your emotions and you'll control your actions, control your actions and you'll control your results."

Enjoy the highs and let them fuel you on to your achievements. However, don't allow your highs to dictate your lows. You should never have extreme emotional volatility. Remember, you hold all the power, you just need to act like it.

Staying Accountable

You created this mess, so it's up to you to take it to success. Yes, you have people in your corner—employees, significant others, family, friends, mentors and cheerleaders, but this all sits squarely upon your shoulders. The more you stay accountable, the stronger those shoulders become. Don't ask "Why me?" because you already know the answer. Somewhere along the line you took your eyes off things and this mess happened. Own it. Embrace it and relish in it.

Being accountable means there are no fingers to point, at others or at you. It is your opportunity and responsibility to drive things to success. Don't shirk that or pass it off; you are the only one who should hold it. That also means when this is done and success has been reached, you can dole out gratitude to others for helping you and staying with you. A piece of those accolades goes to you for staying accountable and making it happen.

Be the Foundation

With this mess comes the opportunity to refortify yourself as the foundation of the company. People will look at you and think, is the foundation going to crumble? It's fine for them to see you, stressed and bending, but ultimately, they need to see that you are the right person for the job. Some of those people will be the ones trying to break the foundation, perhaps unintentionally. You need to be set in your decision to turn the mess into success and not walk away.

Being the foundation means that you take what we've discussed—the emotions, accountability, expectations and everything else that's thrown at you—and manage. Privately you can breakdown, regroup and attack. Outwardly, you need to be the immovable foundation.

Take Time to Think

Deep thinking will allow you to consider new possibilities, refine ideas and gain insight into how you can best manage your situation. Time to think provides time to pause before you react and consider the options you have to solve given challenges. Be quick to think and slow to react. Allow thoughts to enter and leave as they will, gravitating toward those that provide you the best direction. Taking time to pause and think allows emotions to settle and ideas to germinate.

Take Time to Learn

As mentioned in Chapter 7, books are fuel, those that teach and are not just entertaining. Find two or three books that meet your current need for growth, study those and become an expert of that content. Once you have mastered that, find another book that fuels your growth and knowledge.

Prepare to Outlast Everyone

A deeply powerful thought is the knowledge that you will outlast anything and everyone. Know that those who you are dealing with, despite not wanting to, will be gone long after you continue. This will provide you with great power. When you hear people talk about completing something your thoughts should automatically turn to the thought that they only think they get things done, and few can ever match your level of perseverance.

Truly knowing that you will persevere and outlast all will give you the confidence you need to reach success. This knowledge and experience will build your confidence to handle anything, it sets you up nicely to become that healthy narcissist.

Pills

1. How will you know when you've reached success? Can you visualize a moment of when that will be? A moment where you can say that's when it is?
2. Make a list of all the people you need to set clear expectations with. How will you relay to them what you can and cannot do? Make a timeline as to when and how you will reach out to them.
3. How can you prepare yourself to miss the expectations you've set with others? How can you relay that to them without causing alarm?
4. Where can you best take care of yourself? Managing your emotions? Staying accountable? Finding time to think?
5. Visualize what it will feel like when you outlast everyone. Feel what that feels like. Having the resolve and knowledge that you will outlast everyone will drive you.

27 BECOMING A HEALTHY NARCISSIST

We've all heard it said, so and so is a narcissist. It's estimated that roughly one of every 35,000 on the planet have been diagnosed as a narcissist. That means true narcissists are extremely rare, yet everyone knows one. Could it be that what others see as narcissistic is really an individual with a heightened level of self-awareness? Someone that puts their own needs ahead of the desires that another person puts in front of them? As discussed in the previous chapter about eliminating the unnecessary, you will need to put your needs over those of others, risking getting your own label from others as a narcissist. Well, I'm here to tell you that although you don't want the label of narcissist you do want the label of a healthy narcissist.

Being a healthy narcissist means you possess a realistic level of self-esteem without cutting yourself off from those things that bring us a healthy emotional life with those around us. Healthy levels of self-esteem mean that you are self-aware and know your own importance. You also know that your importance is no greater than anyone else's. By putting your needs front and center to create a better life for yourself and others, you are embracing the need to act first for yourself to gain what you most need.

Attributes of a Healthy Narcissist

Healthy narcissists have high levels of self-confidence. It exudes outwardly to the world, but it is in line with reality. They use that self-confidence to push them forward when others stop, and they use it to reset and move forward when needed. They also desire power, wealth and admiration. They pursue this power, but not at all costs. They realize that having power, wealth and admiration does not mean that others can't have it as well. In fact, they want all to have everything they want in life, but they are clearly focused on what they want for their own needs. They have real love and concern for others and their ideas, and do not exploit them. They have a value-based life, and they follow through on their goals, objectives and plans.

Embrace the Healthy Narcissist Inside You

Being humble is an attribute, while being self-deprecating about your abilities is not. There is something admirable when a person holds themselves well and is strong and powerful in their actions over their words. However, in avoiding grandiose displays of your greatness, you should never go the other direction and downplay yourself through self-deprecation. In true narcissistic form, being a healthy narcissist is for your benefit, not others. In turn, being a healthy narcissist helps others.

If you are to reach your highest vision of yourself and make a breakthrough you need to embrace these attributes. Let me ask you this, using my own experiences as an example. Consider which scenario served me and others better?

Scenario one: When I discovered the level of debt we had as a company I spent countless weeks beating myself up, considering my lack of self-worth and where I failed. I approached each debt with apology and a feeling of unworthiness. I was at the creditor's mercy for any level of compassion they could show me so I could have a level of peace.

Scenario two: After I recovered from the bottom level scenario above, I had an awareness. If these people ever wanted to see their money, it would be on my terms. If it wasn't on my terms, they wouldn't see their money. I was unapologetic about this. They were not at my mercy, nor was I at theirs. I didn't need their compassion or even approval, and they needed to stay in their lane and let me do my work. I created my own peace.

At this point in the book you should know how scenario two served me and others. I had developed into a healthy narcissist. That's the message of this book, to move from vulnerable, unsure, unworthy and fearful to secure, sure, worthy and faithful. The goal of this book is to take you from unworthy in your eyes to embracing healthy narcissism. I have felt unworthy and fearful, and it's ugly and doesn't serve anyone. I've also felt healthy narcissism. It's glorious, and it serves myself and others. Let's work to get you there, building a world of healthy narcissists.

Ideas on Building your Healthy Narcissistic Muscle

Visualize your successes. Seeing your direction clearly will give you self-confidence and guidance. Knowing your success, not just believing in it, gives you much needed self-worth.

Become Self-Aware

Carry yourself with a quiet confidence; become comfortable in who you are and where your strengths lie. You don't need to be boisterous, telling people how great you are, but when needed you step up and verbalize that confidence appropriately. You are not perfect, you know your shortcomings and weaknesses, but you don't dwell on them. You focus on your strength, greatness and power. As a self-aware healthy narcissist, you have a healthy ego and a strong desire to learn. You set realistic goals and expectations, then push to exceed them. You know you are a unique, strong and gifted individual, and you have faith in yourself. You also know that others have the same abilities that you possess, and you do your part to help them realize and reach their own greatness.

You Seek Your Own Approval

To reach your highest level and desire for success you realize you must earn it, and also your own approval. You do that by knowing your vision and objectives will become reality, and then by acting and putting into action those things you need to do to make your vision a reality. You don't act with a sense of entitlement; you operate and receive from your actions. You know that the more you risk, the more you fail and ultimately, the greater your reward is. You embrace failure because you know it builds a resiliency muscle and subsequently your success. You inspire yourself to level up and measure up. Although you seek the admiration of others, you seek the approval of yourself.

You are Malleable

Flexibility, being agile and adaptable, allows you to control situations and outcomes. You are in control, which means that when needed, you bend to meet your greater needs. As a mature, healthy narcissist, you know that things change or that another's agenda may mean you are forced to change. When this happens, you know that being malleable means you can shift and negotiate an ideal outcome. You are a problem solver that does so to meet your own goals and objectives. You count on your gut instincts, and the more you do that the more your gut proves to be right. By being malleable you can reach your outcomes while helping others get what's best for them as well.

You are Also Firm

Although malleable, you also know when to be firm and when to pick up the sword and fight. You are okay with this if you know it's right and others needs aren't being stepped upon. But, when a fight is brought to you, you don't run. In fact, you step towards it. You can be firm when you need to be, hard on the outside and cool in the inside. You aren't willing to be taken advantage of and you would never take advantage of another. Your confidence means you won't be bullied, and you don't bully. You protect yourself and those less fortunate.

You Are Charismatic

You understand that your presence and ability to listen with intent to another and give them your full attention makes them feel important and respected. You can give your emotional energy to the person in the moment. You also know that your physical presence, what you are wearing, and the way you stand or sit matters. The more you are present, the more charismatic and charming you are. You know that charisma works for your healthy narcissistic needs while helping others feel important, because you truly know they are.

You Are Respectful

As a healthy narcissist you have respect for yourself first, and others second. You realize that without respect for yourself, others won't respect you and you can't respect others. You know that respect is one of the highest levels of appreciation you can perform. With your healthy ego you can approach business and social activities while knowing that whatever the outcome is, your agreement or acceptance isn't needed for respect to be had. Doing so makes you respected, by others and yourself.

You Are Intelligent

As an intelligent and healthy narcissist, you know that the words that come into your mind or the words that come from your mouth are either beautiful music or venomous poison. The words you choose to tell yourself or to speak to others show your intelligence and ability to control yourself. Your intelligence allows you to avoid the snares that others may set before you and ensures that you won't set them before others or yourself. When you feel frustrated you know to hold yourself accountable and to do an immediate self-assessment, so it meets your narcissistic objectives. You choose not to be reactive; your intelligence allows you to contemplate before responding. You understand that your intelligence and mindfulness not only benefit you, but they benefit others.

Viewing Healthy Narcissism

You may find the use of the word narcissism or all the self-first talk distasteful. However, anything less than speaking and working in the highest state of respect and belief in yourself is a disservice to yourself and others. Remember that the key here is healthy, not just narcissism. Narcissism by itself is equally as bad as being self-loathing. You need to have confidence and a strong belief in your abilities and yourself. You know, given enough time, you can accomplish anything. You live a faith-based life, believing in yourself and your abilities. You are a healthy narcissist.

You Are Powerful

Do you understand now how powerful you are? You are as powerful as you will allow yourself to be. Power is given to you by you. Your mind is the most powerful muscle you have. It can either scare you or it can open you up to the possibilities that life can hold for you. You choose if you are going to overcome and persistently reach out to be your best or if you are going to give in. Life isn't what's making things hard; your unwillingness to push into your power and grow it is. All power, or lack thereof, comes down to your choices.

You Are Ready

It is my belief that you are ready to tackle your fears and challenges, and to rise and meet your hardest demons. When I dragged my sword into battle that was a choice, but it wasn't until later that I realized that all the power I needed to pick up that sword with strength and conviction was already in me. I hope it doesn't take you three years to realize how ready you are, but if it does remember that the journey is worth it. When the power and conviction arrive for you, I hope you will allow me to be there with you. This is real. This is worth it and when you reach it you will look back with a sure knowledge that anything that comes next you can and will handle. You will truly be part of an elite few who can do what you have done.

Remember, you are formidable and capable.

Pills

1. Can you get your head around being a healthy narcissist? How does it feel? Where does it strengthen you? Where does it cause you concern? How do you manage those concerns?
2. How will you go about becoming a healthy narcissist? What will you do and where will you start?
3. Can you remember that you are power, and you are ready? Embrace being a healthy narcissist!

CONCLUSION

As this book is finished the world is in an economic meltdown, a pandemic is in full swing and there is much uncertainty. The feelings I experienced during this current economic decline is similar to what I felt when I had the personal and business economic decline outlined in this book. Now I have company as many people have the same uncertainty. Some worse than others, for some it is a hardship, for others their business has been paused by the government. Fear, doubt and a full-on sense of panic grip many.

The message of this book is hope and direction. All those feelings you have you must conquer and triumph over. You need to gain something for that pain and trouble, it should not be allowed to happen to you without you getting something in return. That something is strength that you have never felt. Growth that you have never experienced. What you are going through is the Refiner's Fire. You can choose to pull yourself out and not learn and grow. You could pull yourself out of everything all together and just say "I'm done, I quit." You can choose not to go through the Refiner's Fire. But you will go through a fire, there will be pain. That much is unavoidable. You could choose to refine a little, to pull yourself out when things start to get a little hot. You can say, "I'm done for a while, this is just too much." But you are left in the state of knowing you could have done more, you should have done more, and you opted out of growth. You can choose to go all in on the Refiner's Fire, feel the heat, get burned and grow like nothing you have imagined. That is where people like you and I choose to live. Not for any other reason but we have no other choice. We see the end in sight, it will not be easy, but it will be glorious. We are not alone, we can build an army.

Remember, you must choose one of two options, you either move forward in fear or faith. Always, we move forward in fear or faith.

Dig in and enjoy the journey.

ABOUT THE AUTHOR

Tab Pierce is the founder and President of Caliber Security Partners. Caliber was created in 2010 and provides cyber security services to enterprise clients and emerging technology companies. He sits on the advisory board of 3P&T Security Recruiting, TraitWare ® and Drug Free Business.

His next venture includes turning the lessons learned from this book into a business. Helping other see that there is a path and that the pathway is glorious and worth the adventure. He hopes you will follow along and join him in an ever-increasing discovery of business, adventure and unification of a global business family lifting each other up as we all seek our own mountain top.

He and his wife Catherine have been married for 33 years, they have four adult children and eight grandchildren with one more on the way. They reside in Mukilteo, Washington, overlooking the Puget Sound. In his free time, he can be found spending it with his three dogs, salmon and halibut fishing, or crabbing out on the Puget Sound. Or working, lots of love for his favorite hobby, business.

References

Robinson, Smokey. "Tears of a Clown". *Make It Happen*. Tamla Records, 1967. Album.

Merle, Andrew. "The Reading Habits of Ultra-Successful People." *HuffPost*, 14 April 2016, https://www.huffpost.com/entry/the-reading-habits-of ult_b_9688130

Star Wars Episode IV: A New Hope. Directed by George Lucas. Twentieth Century Fox, 1977.

Mylett, Ed. "This is the GREATEST THING You Can Do Every Morning!" *YouTube*, 28 Jan 2019, https://www.youtube.com/watch?v=dC67d0lzzAs

Covey, Steven. *The Seven Habits of Highly Effective People*. Free Press, 1989

Made in the USA
Middletown, DE
22 March 2022